WALKING IN THE HAUTE SAVOIE: NORTH

30 DAY WALKS AROUND SALEVE, VALLEE VERTE, ABONDANCE, BELLEVAUX AND MORZINE

About the Author

Janette Norton was born in England but lived near Geneva with her husband Alan for over 40 years, raising four children and working in the marketing and educational fields. Her love of walking and exploring the mountains dated from the time she was a guide in Switzerland in her twenties, and the proximity of both the Alps and the Jura enabled her to continue her passion. After writing her first book on the Haute Savoie, she moved further afield to explore other areas of France, such as Provence, the Cevennes and the Dordogne. Sadly Janette died from cancer in January 2013, and her books are now revised by Alan Norton and Pamela Harris.

Alan Norton studied Physics at Edinburgh and Oxford universities before moving to Geneva to work at CERN on Particle Physics research. Since retirement, he has continued to participate in CERN experiments as a professor at the Italian University of Ferrara. As leisure activities, he has completed many mountain running events at the rear of the field, and helped Janette with walking and map preparation for her guides.

Pamela Harris graduated from Reading University and then moved to Switzerland, where she taught English and Classical studies at international schools in the Geneva area. A long-time member of both the Alpine Club and the Swiss Alpine Club, she has walked and climbed extensively in the mountains of Europe and the Himalayas. For several years she walked with Janette and assisted with previous editions of her guides.

Other Cicerone guides by the author
Walking in the Haute Savoie: South
Walking in Provence: East
Walking in Provence: West
Walking in the Cevennes
Walking in the Dordogne

WALKING IN THE HAUTE SAVOIE: NORTH

30 DAY WALKS AROUND SALEVE, VALLEE VERTE, ABONDANCE, BELLEVAUX AND MORZINE

by Janette Norton

Revised by Alan Norton and Pamela Harris

JUNIPER HOUSE, MURLEY MOSS,
OXENHOLME ROAD, KENDAL, CUMBRIA LA9 7RL
www.cicerone.co.uk

Printed by KHL Printing, Singapore
A catalogue record for this book is available from the British Library.
All photographs are by the author unless otherwise stated.

 Route mapping by Lovell Johns www.lovelljohns.com.
Additional mapping by Alan Norton.

Contains OpenStreetMap.org data © OpenStreetMap
contributors, CC-BY-SA. NASA relief data courtesy of ESRI

FFRandonnée 🏃 The routes of the GR®, PR® and GRP® paths in this guide
www.ffrandonnee.fr have been reproduced with the permission of the Fédération
Française de la Randonnée Pédestre holder of the exclusive
rights of the routes. The names GR®, PR® and GRP® are registered trademarks.
© FFRP 2017 for all GR®, PR® and GRP® paths appearing in this work:

Acknowledgements

It is a daunting task to revise a guidebook when the original author is no longer present to share her skills and experience. Fortunately Janette left us perfect records, as well as wonderful memories, making it a pleasure to pick up her legacy. Even so, we would not have managed without several friends who enthusiastically re-visited some of the trails, providing text updates, GPS traces and brilliant new photographs.

We are especially indebted to Sharon Bryand, Richard Saynor and William Westermeyer, who took charge of the more challenging routes. Thanks also to those who accompanied them or us on various occasions: Patrick Bryand, Kevin Bryand, Carol Saynor, Rosie Westermeyer, Philip Jenkins, Mark Warren, Mike Goodyer, Rebecca Norton, Katherine Heery and Diane Mueller.

It is a pleasure to work with Cicerone, a very special company: cosily small, efficient and demanding when needed, but above all human and understanding when it matters most.

Finally, we are extremely grateful for the information provided by the various tourist offices in the Haute Savoie.

Front cover: Cornettes de Bise in early autumn (Walk 21): photo Richard Saynor

CONTENTS

Symbols used on route maps

			Relief in metres
~	route		
-~-	alternative route		2400–2600
(SF)	start/finish point		2200–2400
(F)	alternative finish point		2000–2200
	woodland		1800–2000
	urban areas		1600–1800
	international border		1400–1600
			1200–1400
▲	peak		1000–1200
♠	refuge		800–1000
■	building		600–800
♦♦	chapel/monastery		400–600
)(	col		200–400
			0–200

Contour lines are drawn at 25m intervals and highlighted at 100m intervals.

GPX files

GPX files for all routes can be downloaded for free at www.cicerone.co.uk/810/gpx

---

Updates to this Guide

While every effort is made by our authors to ensure the accuracy of guidebooks as they go to print, changes can occur during the lifetime of an edition. Any updates that we know of for this guide will be on the Cicerone website (www.cicerone.co.uk/810/updates), so please check before planning your trip. We also advise that you check information about such things as transport, accommodation and shops locally. Even rights of way can be altered over time. We are always grateful for information about any discrepancies between a guidebook and the facts on the ground, sent by email to updates@cicerone.co.uk or by post to Cicerone, Juniper House, Murley Moss, Oxenholme Road, Kendal, Cumbria LA9 7RL, United Kingdom.

Register your book: To sign up to receive free updates, special offers and GPX files where available, register your book at www.cicerone.co.uk.

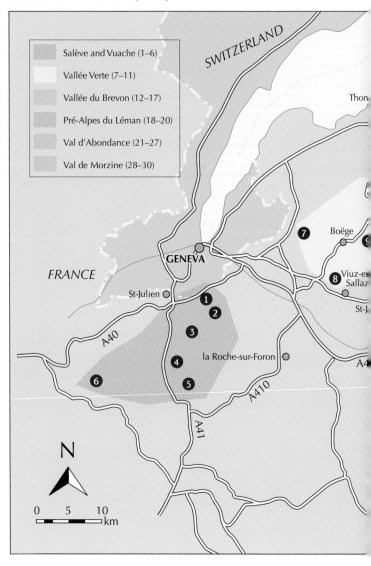

Salève and Vuache (1–6)

Vallée Verte (7–11)

Vallée du Brevon (12–17)

Pré-Alpes du Léman (18–20)

Val d'Abondance (21–27)

Val de Morzine (28–30)

SWITZERLAND

Thon

FRANCE

GENEVA

St-Julien

Boëge

Viuz-e
Sallaz

St-J

la Roche-sur-Foron

A40

A410

A41

A4

N

0   5   10
km

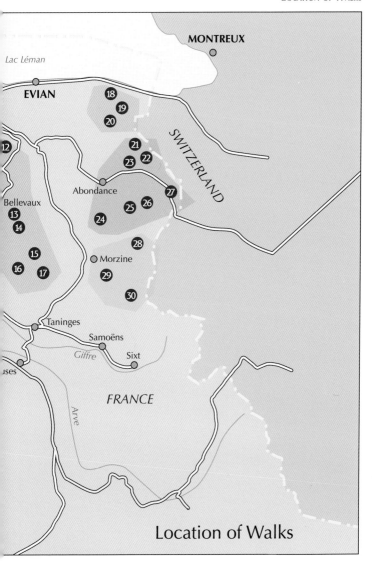

Location of Walks

Lac de Montriond from the Col de Chésery (Walk 28)

PREFACE TO THE THIRD EDITION

Since moving to the Geneva area about 50 years ago, the mountains of the Haute Savoie have been part of our lives. In good weather the Môle and the Salève are always visible across the lake, with the peaks of the Chablais behind and the glistening snows of Mont Blanc towering over all. It is a view we will never tire of, and the walks in this guide lead visitors into the spectacular beauty of what has become our home.

As revisers, we have had great pleasure in preparing this new edition and in re-discovering the delights of the walks we did in our younger days. In the past two years all the walks have been re-done by ourselves and helpers, relying on a few younger – and faster – friends in the case of the more challenging ones.

Although the walking takes longer as the years pass, route finding has become easier, for new signposts and information boards have sprung up almost everywhere. As a result all the route descriptions needed updating, and an increase in building has necessitated the re-routing of some walks or finding a more suitable parking place at the start. Two walks have been suppressed and even lovelier new ones added in their place.

The general introduction has been revised and the walks re-structured into six sections, each with its own introduction. Each walk is accompanied by a new sketch map which overlays a recorded GPS track and key features on a colourful Cicerone base map, and by a profile plot which shows the steepness of the uphill and downhill sections. In addition, the many new photos will illustrate to readers the variety and beauty of this region which we have grown to love so much.

Alan Norton and Pamela Harris

Janette Norton descending from the Col de Planchamp (Walk 20)

INTRODUCTION

Mont Blanc and the peaks of Chablais from Mont Forchat (Walk 11): photo Richard Saynor

Most people associate the French Alps with the town of Chamonix, dominated by Mont Blanc, the highest mountain in Western Europe, and the dazzling array of challenging peaks that surround it. Visitors flock to the Chamonix area to walk and explore, but they do not always realise that the Mont Blanc range is only part of the Haute Savoie. Not far away there are dozens of other interesting mountains and villages to discover, less frequented, steeped in history, and crisscrossed with delightful walking trails.

The Haute Savoie is located in eastern France, bordering Switzerland and Italy. To the north is Lake Geneva (known to the French as Lac Léman), to the southeast is Chamonix, and to the southwest is Lake Annecy. The area in the northeast, which extends into Switzerland, is known as the Chablais, and was originally a separate province. Running for 100km through the centre of the region is the River Arve, rising in the glaciers of the Mont Blanc range and flowing northwest through the towns of Sallanches, Cluses, Bonneville and Annemasse to join the River Rhône and the lake at Geneva. This is the major artery of the region, with the motorway known as

Looking up to the Col de Foron (Walk 15)

the autoroute blanche running alongside to eventually go through the Mont Blanc Tunnel into Italy, an important link between north and south Europe. To the north of the Arve is another east–west artery, the River Giffre, rising in the snowfields of Mont Ruan and flowing through Sixt and Samoëns to join the Arve above Cluses.

This is one of the most mountainous regions in France, with the lower mountains of the Chablais in the north rising to the high peaks of the Mont Blanc range in the south. The walks all give spectacular views, and the trails are well marked and easy to follow. Walks around Chamonix are not included as they are covered in Cicerone's *Mont Blanc Walks*, by Hilary Sharp.

The walks in *Walking in the Haute Savoie: North* are located near to Lake Geneva, beginning with those

on the Salève and Vuache in the west. The remainder are all in the Chablais, a large mountainous area stretching south of the lake and eastwards into Switzerland, which has been divided into the following sections: the Vallée Verte around Boège; the Vallée du Brevon around Bellevaux; the Pré-Alpes du Léman above Evian; and the two main valleys of the River Dranse: the Val d'Abondance and Val de Morzine.

The walks in the companion volume *Walking in the Haute Savoie: South* are mostly located south of the Giffre and Arve rivers. They are situated along the Vallée de l'Arve and above the Plateau d'Assy nearer to Chamonix; in the Vallée du Haut Giffre near Sixt and Samoëns; in the Chaîne des Aravis near La Clusaz and Thônes; on the Plateau de la Borne near la Roche-sur-Foron; and near the shores of Lac d'Annecy.

A SHORT HISTORY OF THE HAUTE SAVOIE

The department of the Haute Savoie did not come into being until 1860 when Napoleon III and King Vittorio-Emmanuele signed the Treaty of Turin, and the Duchy of Savoie, along with Kingdom of Nice, was annexed to France. The area of the Duchy was then split into Haute Savoie, the upper or northern region, and Savoie, the southern region.

The history of the region goes back to prehistoric times when it was

The ruined castle at Chaumont (Walk 6)

settled by Stone Age hunters and farmers. These were succeeded in the sixth century BC by the Celtic Allobroges, who in 121BC were conquered by the Romans. The region became part of the province of Gallia Narbonensis, and it was a Roman historian who in AD380 made the first written reference to Savoie, calling it Sabaudia, 'land of the fir trees'. After the Fall of the Roman Empire the Germanic tribe of Burgundians moved in, and a series of chieftains governed until AD1003 when Humbert the 'White-Handed' was made the first count of Savoie. The counts were vassals of the Holy Roman Emperors, who in the ensuing years granted them even more territory, their lands eventually stretching from Lake Geneva in the north, including parts of western Switzerland, to the Dauphiné in the south, with their capital at Chambéry. The power of the counts was based on their control of the Alpine passes, and feudal castles were built at strategic sites to protect their lands.

In 1416 the Holy Roman Emperor made the County of Savoie an independent Duchy, with Amadée VIII as its first duke, and in 1429 this was unified with Piedmont in northwest Italy, its territory now stretching as far south as Nice. The dukes had considerable power and influence, and in an age of great religious belief had a number of abbeys and monasteries built. One of those still standing is the Abbaye d'Abondance. The remote mountain valleys provided

Abondance Abbey cloisters

an ideal retreat for Carthusian monks who wished for seclusion, and the Chartreuse du Reposoir in the Aravis still remains, although now it belongs to the Carmelites.

For a time there was peace in the region, but at the start of the 16th century the Protestant Reformation under Calvin spread from Geneva and Catholicism was outlawed, resulting in many deaths. It was a young priest, François de Sales, born in 1567 near the village of Thorens-Glières, who managed to convert the population back to the Catholic faith. He has been revered by the local population as a saint ever since, and many small chapels, wayside shrines and statues have been erected in his memory, especially in the Vallée Verte and the Val d'Abondance, where a fragment of his elbow bone has recently been found.

In the following years the strategic position of Savoie meant that it continued to be a battleground for the powers of France and Austria as they fought over it, first one side and then the other gaining control. In addition, both the Chablais in the northeast and the Geneva area in the northwest were taken over for a short time by the Swiss. Then, in 1714, as a result of the War of the Spanish Succession, Savoie gained the Kingdom of Sicily, which in 1720 was exchanged for that of Sardinia. From now on the heads of the House of Savoie were known as the Kings of Piedmont-Sardinia, and their capital moved to Turin.

Although the area was still very poor and many of the peasants had emigrated, some prosperity was coming to the region as industries began to develop, with clock- and watchmaking in the Arve valley and stonemasonry in the Haut Giffre. In addition, as the beauty of the Alpine scenery was discovered by writers and painters of the Romantic movement, the area gradually opened up to tourists. The first ascent of Mont Blanc in 1786 by Balmat and Paccard was the start of the Age of Alpinism, and soon Chamonix and its glaciers were on the list of places visited by aristocratic young men on their Grand Tour of Europe.

When the French Revolution broke out in 1792 France invaded yet again, and Savoie, including Geneva, became part of the department of Mont Blanc, later known as the department of Mont Blanc-Léman. But after the defeat of Napoleon in 1815 the Congress of Vienna ruled that Savoie be given back to the King of Piedmont-Sardinia, although this time the people of Geneva decided to join the Confederation of Swiss States and cut themselves off irrevocably.

This was followed by a relatively prosperous economic and cultural period. Many churches and other buildings date from this time, and the clock-making industry and agriculture became firmly established. French culture and language continued to flourish, until in 1860 Savoie was finally ceded to France and

Vittorio-Emmanuele, the last Duke of Savoie, became the first King of Italy.

Today the Haute Savoie is one of the richest and most developed areas of France. Industry has expanded, the Arve valley being well known for its precision and mechanical engineering, with 1200 companies in a 30km radius. There are many other businesses, such as the manufacture of ski equipment, and wood related industries such as forestry and furniture making. Since 1965 the Mont Blanc road tunnel has provided an important link between France in the north and Italy in the south, thus placing the Haute Savoie on one of the greatest trade routes in Europe.

More importantly, tourism has grown exponentially in the last 50 years, especially since the 1960s when skiing became popular and new resorts such as Flaine and Morzine–Avoriaz were constructed, opening up hundreds of kilometres of ski runs, those of the Portes du Soleil linking with Switzerland. Climbing and walking have also become increasingly popular activities, aided by the building of refuges for overnight stays and the construction of long-distance footpaths that run through the area. The creation of nature reserves has ensured that the beauty of the environment, with its rich wildlife and flora, is protected for posterity.

WILDLIFE

Thanks to the ecology movement and the creation of nature reserves, the animal population of the Alps

The Alpine Museum at the Chalets de Bise (Walk 21)

has increased in recent years. A good example of this is in the Réserve des Aravis, where chamois had been hunted almost to extinction. When the park was created in 1972 there were only six left, whereas now there are over a thousand.

The various species which can be glimpsed, if you are lucky and there are not too many people, are deer, ibex, chamois, moufflons, mountain hares, wild boar, marmots, grouse, buzzards, eagles, ptarmigan and bearded vultures. There are also the more widespread rodents such as foxes, dormice, stoats, weasels, pine martens and squirrels. Both lynx and wolves have recently made a re-appearance in the Haute Savoie, the lynx coming across from Switzerland, where it was re-introduced, and the wolf from the Italian Alps. Both are protected animals, and farmers are concerned about implications for their livestock.

If you are interested in finding out more about the wildlife of the area, the following books are recommended:
Wild Animals of Britain and Europe (Collins Nature Guide)
Birds of Britain & Europe (Collins Pocket Guide)
Butterflies of Europe, Tristan Lafranchis (Diatheo)

Animals
Ibex are mountain goats with beautifully curved ridged horns, sometimes more than a metre long. Sturdy, passive animals, the ibex has no natural enemies, although the babies have been known to make an eagle's meal.

Ibex on the Cornettes de Bise (Walk 21): photo Philip Jenkins

They are usually to be found at an altitude of about 2000m, the females with their young in small family groups, and the males joining them during the rutting season at the end of the year, when they use their long horns to fight off other contenders for their females. The ibex was hunted to extinction in the Alps and only reintroduced in the 1960s, but unfortunately it was discovered in 2013 and again in 2015 that some of the animals had contracted brucellosis, a disease that can be transmitted to livestock and humans. Farmers were concerned about their cattle and about cheese production, and as a result an enormous cull took place, amid much controversy.

The chamois is a daintier, lighter and more agile animal than the ibex, being the alpine representative of the antelope family. With a pretty, striped brown and cream face, the males having two small curving horns, they are often to be seen in large herds leaping from rock to rock in the most inhospitable places, but you will rarely get near them as they are timid and nervous. Their speed and agility is due to their hooves which, like small cushions on normal terrain, have the ability to widen and become like crampons on precipitous rocky slopes. Although chamois can still be hunted, quotas have been strictly controlled since 1982, and hunting is restricted to a few weeks in the autumn.

The moufflon is a species of mountain sheep with thick, scroll-shaped horns. It was first introduced to the alpine regions from Corsica in the 1950s so that it could be hunted and thus solve a food problem. In 1969 about 60 animals were installed in different areas of the Haute Savoie, including in the Réserve Naturelle du Mont de Grange in the Val d'Abondance, and in 1978 a herd was released on the slopes of the Tournette near Annecy. At present there are about 300 in the Haute Savoie, although some ecologists are against animals being introduced into a region where they were never endemic. They are passive, slow animals that spend at least eight hours a day peacefully grazing on the higher slopes.

If you come across a large patch of meadowland where the grass has been churned up and the earth turned over, you know that there are wild-boar in the vicinity. This is not an animal one would choose to meet face to face – which fortunately is unlikely – since they can weigh as much as 150kg and be very aggressive if cornered. They are really just wild pigs that like to live in small herds, mainly in forest areas, and are more numerous in the wooded Jura mountains than the Alps. They have no enemies other than hunters, and their meat, rich and gamey, is considered a great delicacy.

The most charming of all the alpine animals is the marmot, which live in colonies above 1000m. If you hear a piercing whistle echoing across

Marmots emerging from their burrow: photo Carol Saynor

the slopes, stop dead in your tracks and keep your eyes peeled for one of these enchanting creatures, which are usually to be found in rocky grasslands. The whistle is the alarm call from the marmot on sentry duty telling his fellows that there is danger in the vicinity so that they can rush back into their burrows – a single cry warns of an airborne predator, and a series of cries of one on the ground. But they are not really shy creatures, and if you stay quiet, curiosity will overcome their fear and you will see a furry head pop out again to look around and survey the slopes.

During the winter months marmots hibernate in their deep, grass-lined burrows, living off accumulated fat until they emerge thin and hungry in mid-April. The marmot has few enemies, except for eagles who like to snatch the babies, and they have never been seriously hunted for food. They are prolific in the Alps and the walker has a good chance of seeing them on many occasions.

Birds

Of all the alpine birds of prey, the most impressive is the golden eagle, which, having been protected for a number of years, can be seen more frequently. A more recent newcomer is the bearded vulture, which was reintroduced into the Alps in 1978 and of which there are now around 100 couples. In 1987, 19 young birds were introduced into the Haute Savoie, where they are heavily protected. With a wing span of three metres they are an awe-inspiring sight as they circle majestically among the high peaks.

One of the most interesting of birds to be found at around 2000m is the shy ptarmigan. The size of a pigeon, the ptarmigan can only fly for short bursts, preferring to stay on the ground pecking around for grass and berries. In summer its plumage is brown, a perfect camouflage against the rock and scree where between May and July the females will raise from four to eight chicks in a nest in a rocky hollow or long grass.

In winter ptarmigans turn white, merging with the snowy environment, and they protect themselves against the arctic cold by building an igloo in the snow with their claws, where they can remain for days without food. Unfortunately their numbers have been much reduced as they are often disturbed by skiers or caught in the overhead wires of ski lifts. The black grouse, renowned for its mating displays, is another bird that is fast disappearing due to ski installations and being hunted for the pot. It prefers bushy areas at altitudes between 1400m and 2600m.

Alpine choughs are to be found at the top of many a mountain, especially those frequented by picnickers. They are distinguished from the chough by their red legs and short yellow bill rather than a curved red one. They make a sinister, high-pitched screech that is in complete harmony with the precipitous rocky

summits they favour. Look out too for falcons, buzzards, hawks, larks and the smaller birds such as the dipper, which loves to run along the bottom of rushing Alpine torrents at high altitude.

Butterflies

Butterflies can still be found in the meadows, and even at higher altitudes, including those that are now rare in Britain, such as the graceful, creamy yellow and brown swallowtails and the purple Camberwell beauty with its striking cream border. Among the commoner species there are plenty of red admirals, tortoiseshells, yellow brimstones and tiny meadow blues.

PLANTS AND FLOWERS

One of the joys of walking in the mountains, especially in spring and early summer, is the abundance and variety of flowers growing in the Alpine pastures, among rock crevices, and in places where you would think no plant life could possibly take hold. The type of mountain terrain affects the species you will find, some thriving on granite, for example, while others prefer limestone. If you are interested in identifying

Clockwise from top right:
fragrant orchid, yellow bellflower,
alpenrose, soldanella, fairy
foxgloves, alpine daffodils

and knowing the names of the individual species, buy a good flower book and a magnifying lens and keep them permanently in your rucksack, and remember to leave extra time for flower identification.

Some of the first flowers you will see in the year, pushing through the melting snow, are members of the bulb and corm family – thousands of little white and purple alpine crocuses, scillas, snowflakes and gageas. These are closely followed by soldanellas, spring gentians, alpine daffodils, sweet smelling narcissi, alpine anemones, violets, rockroses and the deep blue trumpet gentians.

In May and June come the small, delicate field orchids. The earliest of these are the early purple, which flower in April, and elderflower, the yellow and purple varieties growing side by side. Later you will find fragrant, common spotted, burnt, round-headed, pyramidal, butterfly and military, and in August the black vanilla, which actually smells of vanilla. Rarer ones are the lady orchid, which usually grows further south, the tiny green frog and the lady's slipper, which can be found in isolated places. Most orchids have a spike of flowers, often with a sort of helmet behind, and the lower petal is in the shape of a lip.

In June look out for lilies, the delicate white paradise lily growing on the higher slopes, and the striking deep pink martagon or turk's cap lily in woods or grassland. Common

on high-altitude moorland is the well-known alpenrose (alpine rhododendron), a bushy evergreen shrub with clusters of pale pink to deep pinkish-red flowers, and of course every walker hopes one day to come across the rare edelweiss.

Yellow cowslips, oxlips and primulas are also in abundance, and you will find the pretty, lilac-pink bird's eye primula farinosa growing beside streams and in damp places. The prolific creamy and yellow pulsatilla anemones and yellow globe flowers strike a vivid note on the green slopes, and the banks of the swollen rivulets cascading down the mountainsides are sprinkled with bright yellow marsh marigolds.

Brightening up bare crevices and clinging to inaccessible rock faces are dozens of different creeping, cushiony rock plants which have lots of tiny blooms, such as saxifrages, moss campion, globularia, toadflax and rock jasmines.

As the slopes are warmed by spring sunshine and the snows start to melt in earnest, more and more flowers appear. July and August are the time for taller plants, with lesser known varieties of gentians coming into flower, such as the great yellow gentian, from whose root the gentian liqueur is made, and a little later, spotted and willow-leaved. There are tall purple monkshood and delphiniums, graceful columbines, rosebay willow herb, meadow cranesbills, and various types of the carrot family, including cow parsley and the star-like astrantia. There are endless varieties of daisies, including the orange splash of the golden hawksbeard, purple asters and fluffy lilac adenostyles, and dozens of different white and purple thistles with their prickly, silvery leaves. The white false helleborine, a tall yellowish-green starred flower, is frequently found around alpine chalets as it likes the nitrogen-enriched soil. Cattle never touch its poisonous leaves, although these were formerly picked and made into a potion to be used against lice and horseflies.

Many flowers continue to bloom until the end of September and even into October. In these months you will still find harebells and other varieties of the campanula family, and if you are lucky you may spot the rare yellow bellflower (*campanula thyrsoides*). Small purple field gentians and bright blue fringed gentians now cover the slopes, both distinguished from the earlier spring flowering variety by having only four petals instead of five. Look out for tiny delicate cyclamens in the woods, autumn crocuses (*colchicum*) in the fields, and heather higher up.

In many tourist offices and mountain refuges there are posters indicating which alpine flowers are rare and therefore protected, and in the nature reserves there are signs stating clearly that it is forbidden to pick any flowers, and certainly not to dig them up. There is nothing more beautiful than

Autumn colours below the Pointe des Mattes (Walk 26)

a meadow of wildflowers, especially the alpine daffodils or narcissi that can cover an entire mountainside, and nothing more heart breaking than seeing people walking along with bunches of wilted flowers in their hands.

In late autumn the flowers die away, but the colour continues with bright red rowan berries and the changing leaves, with some magnificent displays of reds and yellows from beech, maple and larch. There are wild raspberries and bilberries for the picking, and in wooded areas there is also a fascinating range of fungi, the edible ones being a real French delicacy. Some of these are quite unlike any found in Britain – they are white, black, grey, purple and even a chilling green – and can normally be seen clinging to the roots of trees or hidden under mounds of dead leaves. There is also the big round red variety

with white spots that reminds one of fairytales. Many of these fungi are highly poisonous and should never be eaten without checking first at a local *pharmacie* (chemist), where there is usually an expert who will do this willingly.

For more information about the plants and flowers of the area, consult *Alpine Flowers of Britain & Europe*, by Christopher Grey-Wilson and Marjorie Blamey (Collins). You might also like *Alpine Flowers* by Gillian Price (Cicerone), a useful pocket guide.

GETTING THERE

By car
Many of the walks in this book cannot be reached without a car. If you come by train or air, all the main car hire firms operate from stations and

The Dents du Midi from the Col de Cou (Walk 30)

airports, and information about rental can be obtained before you leave.

If you bring your own car, it is better to avoid Paris and take the motorway from Calais via Reims, Chalons, Troyes and Dijon to either Geneva or Annecy. For detailed travel itineraries and route planners, see www.theaa.com, www.rac.co.uk and www.viamichelin.com.

By air

With the increase of cheap flights, flying and then hiring a car can be a more convenient way to travel. The nearest airport to the Haute Savoie is Geneva, and many of the walks in this guide are within an hour's drive of the city. EasyJet flies to Geneva several times a day from various UK airports (www.easyjet.co.uk), as do British Airways (www.britishairways.com), Swiss (www.swiss.com) and Flybe (www.flybe.com).

If you hire a car from Geneva Airport, check the situation with your rental company or arrange to do so from the French side as recently introduced regulations may prohibit cars hired in Switzerland from being taken into EU countries.

By rail

If you contact the English office of the French Railways at RailEurope (www.raileurope.com), they will send an informative brochure outlining the different ways to get to France by rail, including timetables, cost, car hire and so on.

There are frequent high-speed trains with Eurostar to Lille or Paris, where you can catch a TGV train to arrive in Geneva in three hours or Annecy in four hours. For further information, including online booking, timetables, destinations and costs contact www.eurostar.com. Another useful website for European train travel is www.seat61.com (just click on France).

WHEN TO GO

The Haute Savoie climate is more continental than temperate Britain, which means the winters are colder and the summers hotter. However, mountains generate their own weather, and you can be in brilliant sunshine lower down and climb up into dense cloud and even rain as you get higher. It is always important to check the local weather forecast before setting off on a walk.

Since some of the walks in this guide are at lower altitudes, they can be done as early as May or June, when the weather can be warm and sunny and the days start to lengthen. Another advantage to this time is that many of the alpine flowers are in full bloom, and there are fewer tourists. However, be careful to choose a suitable walk as there can still be snow on the northern slopes or at higher altitudes until the beginning of July in some years.

Snow lingering into springtime at the Col d'Ubine (Walk 23): photo Richard Saynor

The best time for walking anywhere in the Alps is from mid-June to mid-September, when it is often hot and sunny and the days are longer. The snow will have melted from the upper trails, the lifts are working, the mountain refuges are open, and the slopes are covered with flowers. However, the weather cannot be relied on to be always sunny, and you can have day after day of rain, and sometimes heavy thunderstorms, especially in the afternoons. The busiest holiday period is mid-July to mid-August, and it is wise to book accommodation in advance at this time.

Another good period is September and October, when the school holidays are over and there are fewer tourists. The weather can still be warm and sunny and is often more stable, with a clarity in the air that makes the views even more magnificent. The glory of the spring flowers may be over, but you are compensated by the trees turning an autumn gold, with a variety of brightly coloured berries.

Often the sunny weather continues into November, and if the snow has not come early, it is still possible to do many of these walks. However, remember that the days are drawing in so there is less walking time, and that rocks can be slippery in the morning if the sun has only just reached them. There is something particularly magical about walking in late autumn for, with the cloud inversion over Lake Geneva, you can drive up out of the gloom into brilliant sunshine and be looking down on to a mass of 'cotton wool' covering the valley below. Other peaks stick up like islands, and the permanently snow-covered higher ranges

Cloud inversion in late autumn (Walk 19)

such as Mont Blanc look even more impressive with their lower slopes cloaked in fog. If you are walking at this time, be careful to find out where the cloud level is as sometimes it can be quite high and you can be walking all day with the sunshine just a few metres above, if you but knew it.

ACCOMMODATION

There is plenty of accommodation all over the Haute Savoie, ranging from four-star hotels to campsites and mountain refuges. July and August are high season, so if you plan to walk then it is advisable to book in advance. The local tourist offices will often provide a list of available accommodation and help you to book. See Appendix B for a list of websites.

Hotels

The larger towns such as Geneva or Annecy have numerous hotels of all categories to choose from, whereas the smaller villages will have just a few. In addition, ski resorts have begun to keep their hotels open in the summer months as well, widening the choice of where to stay. A reliable chain of hotels offering comfortable accommodation at reasonable prices is Logis de France, which has about 200 hotels in the Haute Savoie (www.logishotels.com).

Gîtes and chambres d'hôtes

There is also plenty of self-catering accommodation to rent in *gîtes* (www.gites-de-france-haute-savoie.com), and the same website gives information on *chambres d'hôtes*, the French equivalent of bed and breakfast. *Gîtes*

29

d'étape offer basic lodging, often in dormitory accommodation, and provide meals (www.gites-refuges.com).

Camping

Campsites are graded from one to five stars and range from those offering shop, hot showers and swimming pool to sites with basic washing facilities. A list is available at www.campingsavoie.com/liste/haute-savoie.htm.

Refuges (mountain huts)

Details of the refuges on specific walks are given in the route descriptions. Some are run by the French Alpine Club, but many are privately owned. These refuges are often above 2000m and are mainly used by serious walkers and climbers as a base for

tackling higher peaks. Most have only communal dormitories, but some provide rooms for two or four. There are always toilets and running water, and some even provide hot showers.

Most huts are open from mid-June to mid-September when there will be a guardian in residence who provides an evening meal and breakfast for a reasonable price. The days when climbers carried up their own food to cook are long gone! If you intend to spend an overnight in a hut, it is essential to make a booking in advance as there is limited space.

SAVOYARD FOOD AND DRINK

The food of the Haute Savoie is centred round its local products, the most

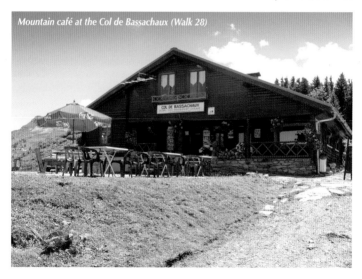

Mountain café at the Col de Bassachaux (Walk 28)

important of these being cheese. The lush grass of the alpine pastures provides excellent grazing for dairy cattle, the best known being the brown and white Abondance cows. Now found throughout the Haute Savoie, they originated in the valley of the same name, and their cheese has been made since the 14th century. Taking three months to ripen, it is a fairly hard, golden coloured cheese, with a nutty flavour.

Tomme de Savoie is a popular cheese made everywhere in Savoie. It is mild and semi-firm, with a low fat content, made from skimmed milk.

Chevrotin is a soft cheese made from goat's milk and has been produced in the Aravis area for generations. It is formed in small rounds, and is ripe and ready to eat after only three weeks of maturing in a cellar.

Reblochon cheese is a speciality of the Aravis region around Thônes and le Grand Bornand, and was first mentioned in the 16th century when it was much appreciated by the court of Piedmont-Sardinia, as it could travel all the way to Turin without getting spoilt. The name comes from the French word *la rôblosse*, meaning second milking, and dates back to the time when all the land and cattle belonged to the church, and the peasants were taxed on the amount of milk they produced. They used to trick the monks by pretending they had finished milking the cows and then, as soon as the monks were out of sight, they would do a second milking,

which was the richest and creamiest, producing a smooth, mild cheese.

Cheese can also be melted to make *fondue* or *raclette*, frequently served on ski holidays in the French Alps, but a less well-known dish is *tartiflette*. Made from Reblochon cheese, it consists of layers of cooked potatoes garnished with onion and slivers of bacon and then covered with a whole cheese, the rind uppermost. It is then put under the grill until the cheese is crusty and bubbling – worth trying. Cheese platters are often accompanied by dried or smoked meats, and by nuts or locally grown fruit such as apples, pears and figs.

There are several varieties of freshwater fish to be found, such as trout, pike, crayfish, perch and the *omble chevalier*, a species of arctic char found mainly in deep mountain waters such as Lac d'Annecy, but now also artificially farmed near Thonon.

In autumn you will often see locals collecting mushrooms and picking berries, and *tarte aux myrtilles*, a delicious bilberry tart, is sometimes on offer in a mountain refuge. Another local speciality is *matafan*, a thick pancake which can be eaten with salt or sugar.

The white wines of Savoie are an excellent accompaniment to cheese or fish dishes, with Chasselas, Crépy, Ripaille and Roussette to choose from, the latter from a type of vine originating in Cyprus and brought to the Frangy-Seyssel region at the time of the Crusades. After a meal it is worth

Roussette de Frangy wine (Walk 6)

trying a locally made *digestif* such as *génépi*, a herbal liqueur made from the dried leaves of the wormwood plant, or *eau de vie de gentiane*, made from the roots of the yellow gentian flower. And last but not least are the renowned mineral waters from the towns of Thonon and Evian-les-Bains.

You will find regional produce in local markets, which are great fun to wander round even if you have no intention of buying, and local cheeses can often be bought directly from the farms you pass on the walks. See Appendix B for market days.

WHAT TO TAKE

As with all mountainous regions, the weather in the Haute Savoie can change rapidly without warning, and a careful choice of clothing and equipment is essential for your safety and security. The best solution is to dress in layers and to carry a light fleece and a waterproof anorak, even if the forecast is good. Lightweight, quick-drying trousers are the most comfortable for walking – those that zip down into shorts are very practical, as even on hot days you may need long trousers to avoid getting scratched by undergrowth. Protection against the sun is important, especially at higher altitudes where ultraviolet rays are more intense.

The most important piece of equipment for mountain walking is a pair of comfortable boots, with ankle support and Vibram-type soles with a good tread. Proper walking socks can also make an enormous difference to foot comfort.

For day walks, a light 20–30-litre rucksack is sufficient, with a padded back and waist strap, and with side and top pockets for small items. Some of the larger trekking rucksacks have a big top pocket, which can be detached and used as a day pack. Many rucksacks now come with a waterproof cover, or these can be bought separately.

Trekking poles are now used by almost everyone when mountain walking, and are especially useful in helping with balance on rough terrain and taking stress off the knees on steep descents. The lightest available are made of carbon fibre, and lever-lock adjustments are the easiest to use.

A whistle and a good-quality compass are essential in the mountains, and an altimeter and GPS are useful in bad weather or if you get lost. A mobile phone can be life-saving if you have an accident. Unfortunately, the more remote mountain areas are often out of network coverage.

There has been no let-up in the evolution of GPS technology over the past 20 years, with increased power of sophisticated hand-held units, including custom maps for downloading, and access to more satellites (including Russian ones). Although you should always carry a quality compass, many GPS units now incorporate a compass and an altimeter, based on barometric pressure and/or satellite trigonometry.

It is worth checking the market carefully before purchasing a GPS unit, putting the accent on good signal reception and battery life, good screen visibility in bright light, easy operation, robust and not too large and heavy. There is also a learning

Cornettes de Bise from the Col de Vernaz (Walk 22)

curve, but the effort is well-rewarded and Pete Hawkin's Cicerone guide *Navigating with a GPS* gives a useful introduction.

Manufacturers' maps for GPS download are usually very expensive, and the French IGN 1:25,000 products are no exception. However, there are open software products that are surprising effective and versatile, with special mention for openmtbmap.org ('mtb' covers mountain biking and hiking).

EQUIPMENT LIST

The following is a suggested list for your rucksack on a day walk:
- the route description from this walking guide
- the IGN 1:25,000 map recommended in the walk information box
- waterproof anorak
- cape or poncho to cover everything, including your rucksack – useful when it is really pouring, and for sitting on
- lightweight fleece or sweater
- warm hat, gloves and scarf (in cold weather)
- spare socks
- sun hat, sunglasses, high factor sun cream and lipsalve
- basic first-aid kit, including insect repellent and moleskin for blisters
- survival blanket
- picnic and snacks (sweets, chocolate, high energy bars, dried fruit and nuts)
- water bottle – it is essential to take plenty of water; avoid drinking from mountain streams or dubious drinking troughs and fountains
- mobile phone, whistle, torch, penknife, compass, altimeter
- optional extras: GPS, camera, binoculars, reference books (for flowers or birds)

If you are staying overnight in a refuge, add the following:
- wash gear and small towel
- change of clothes
- sheet sleeping bag (silk ones are the lightest); all the refuges in the Haute Savoie provide blankets
- a head torch is very useful (especially if there is only an outside toilet)
- tracksuit for relaxing in the evening and for sleeping in
- lightweight trainers (most refuges provide hut shoes but this is not guaranteed)
- playing cards and/or book – in case you are holed up by bad weather
- small repair kit with needles, thread, string, buttons, etc.

WAYMARKING

Most of the walks in the Haute Savoie, as in other areas in France, have been newly waymarked with pale yellow plastic signposts. These have a heading specifying the location of the signpost and/or an altitude, and clearly show the various destinations and times taken to get there. These are used as points of reference in the route descriptions. There are also green plastic squares with yellow arrows, either nailed to posts or on trees. In some places the original wooden signposts remain, and you will still find some faded coloured paint splashes, mostly yellow.

Quite a number of walks in the Haute Savoie are partly along sections of long-distance Grande Randonnée (GR) footpaths, which are linear, and on the walks in this guide you will come across the GR5, the GR65 and the GR Balcon du Léman. These are marked by red and white horizontal stripes on posts, rocks or trees, as well as on signposts, with a red and white cross to indicate the wrong direction.

The GR5 starts from the small town of St Gingolph on Lake Geneva, with an alternative start at Thonon-les-Bains, and goes all the way to Nice. After skirting Mont d'Hermone from Thonon and Dent d'Oche from St Gingolph, the two branches converge to pass through the Val d'Abondance and Val de Morzine, continue into the Vallée du Haut Giffre to the Lac d'Anterne, and then

An example of a new signpost (Walk 26)

Chalet de La Torrens
alt. 1735 m

Les Mattes — 0 h 40
L'Etrye — 1 h 20
Lenlevay — 2 h

0 h 15 — Les Québales
1 h 05 — Les Boudimes
2 h — Très-les-Pierres par Les Boudimes

head south to Chamonix and on to the Mediterranean.

The GR65 follows the ancient pilgrimage route from Geneva and the Salève to le Puy and on to Santiago de Compostela in Spain.

The GR Balcon du Léman follows the mountain crests round the French part of Lake Geneva, passing through the Vuache, Salève, Vallée Verte and Pré-Alpes du Léman.

In addition to the GR footpaths, there are Grande Randonnée de Pays (GRP or GR de Pays) footpaths, which are long circuits marked by red and yellow horizontal stripes. You will come across two of them in this guide: the Tour de la Vallée Verte and the Tour des Crêtes de Bellevaux.

Where the route for a walk is on a GR or a GRP footpath, this is clearly indicated in both the text and on the accompanying sketch map.

At the start of many walks the local tourist offices have erected large information boards, which are mentioned in the text of individual walks. These usually show a map of walks; a panorama of peaks; pictures of animals, birds and flowers; and anything of historical or geological interest in the area. They are often in English as well as French, and it is worth taking the time to read them before setting off.

MAPS

Each walk is accompanied by a sketch map with coloured contours, showing key places and numbered waypoints that are highlighted in the route description. For additional features and detailed navigation, the relevant 1:25,000 IGN paper map is specified in the information box at the beginning of each walk. However, bear in mind that things are still changing in this region, and you may discover new ski lifts, roads or jeep tracks that are not yet on the maps.

A good map that gives an overall picture of the Haute Savoie walking areas is the IGN Top 100 Tourisme et Découverte No.144 Annecy/Thonon-les-Bains, 1:100,000.

A complete list of IGN maps can be found in Appendix B, together with details of where to buy or order them in the UK. Otherwise, it is usually easy to buy them in the region and they are sometimes cheaper in local supermarkets.

For pre-walk planning and post-analysis, all the 1:25,000 and 1:100,000 IGN maps for the whole of France are available on the internet for a very small annual subscription from www.sitytrail.com. This is the best way to be sure you have the latest editions, and is accompanied by a powerful set of tools to choose the magnification, print selected areas, superimpose recorded GPS trails and record your favourite routes online. The sitytrail subscription includes access to the same maps with a tablet or smartphone App. For offline use, especially along walking trails, it is possible to download a set of map tiles for a local area. Note that sitytrail maps are also available for Switzerland with a separate subscription.

There are numerous Apps on the market that offer GPS tracking with open software maps. On the iPhone or iPad, MOTIONX-GPS is particularly convenient and flexible.

GPX files for all the routes described here are available to anyone who has bought this guide to download free from the Cicerone website. Just go to www.cicerone.co.uk/810/GPX.

SAFETY

When heading off on any of the walks, always let at least one person know where you are going and the time which you expect to return, and log the following emergency numbers into your mobile:

General emergency number for the whole of France: 112.

Mountain rescue in the Haute Savoie: +33 450 53 16 89.

Here are some other important walking rules:

- Read the route description carefully and look at the map before you set off.
- Give yourself plenty of time by setting off early.
- Check the weather forecast before you leave, and do not set out if there is a danger of fog, storms or snow.
- Keep on the marked path – if there is a short cut, it is usually

shown. If you get lost, go back the way you came if possible. Avoid going across patches of scree or snow, and watch out for slippery grassy slopes.

- Be careful when crossing pastures with cows or sheep, as cows can attack when they have calves, and sheep are often guarded by large white pastous dogs, which are trained to defend their flock.
- Be careful not to dislodge stones or boulders – they can gather momentum as they roll down the mountain and hit other walkers.
- Be sure that you have enough warm clothes and food, and plenty of water if it is a hot day.
- If you are not used to the sun at altitude, remember to put on a high-protection sunscreen and to wear reliable sunglasses.
- Never walk alone, even if you know the route.
- If you get caught in a thunderstorm, get off high, exposed ground immediately and take shelter, but not under an isolated tree or rock. If lightning strikes, remove any metallic objects you might have on you and, if necessary, curl up on the ground to avoid being struck.
- If there is an accident, wrap the person concerned in a survival blanket. Use your whistle – six short blasts means you need help (three short ones means you are all right), or six flashes from your torch if it is dark. If you have to

Peaks of the Chablais from Pic des Mémises (Walk 18)

leave to get help, make sure you know where you are located and leave as much warm clothing and food with the victim as possible.

- Remember that these mountains are a cultural heritage and should be left unspoilt for future generations – happy walking!

USING THIS GUIDE

The 30 walks in this guidebook are grouped into six sections: Salève and Vuache, Vallée Verte, Vallée du Brevon, Pré-Alpes du Léman, Val d'Abondance and Val de Morzine. Each section starts with an introduction to the area covered in the walks that follow, with a few towns and villages mentioned as convenient places to stay. At the beginning of the route description for each walk there is a box giving a range of useful information: the start and finish of the walk; distance; figures for total ascent and maximum altitude; a difficulty grading and an approximation of time (see further below); the relevant maps; access information to reach the start point; and signposting encountered on the walk. This information is also summarised in a route summary table in Appendix A. Throughout the route descriptions place names and features that are shown on the map are highlighted in **bold** and facilities that are passed are highlighted.

Walk grading

None of the walks in this book go higher than 2450m and many of them are considerably lower. As a simple guide, they are graded as follows:

- Easy: these are short walks on good well-marked paths, with a total ascent of less than 500m. Some can be done in a half day.
- Medium: these are longer walks with a total ascent of up to 800m, also on well-marked paths. They generally need most of a day.
- Strenuous: these walks are more demanding, involving longer distances and a total ascent of over 800m. They require a full day of up to eight hours.

- Difficult: these are also long, with a total ascent of over 800m, but in addition have some steep and exposed sections requiring a head for heights, or entail some scrambling, often with the help of chains or cables.

A very useful indicator is the profile plot of altitude versus distance for each walk, which shows the distribution and steepness of the various uphill and downhill sections. The total ascent is the sum of the height gains for all the uphill stretches, by definition equal to the total descent for a circular walk. As a guideline, with a light rucksack you should be able to climb 300m in one hour, with a faster descent. The altitudes in the profile

Walking along the ridge to Pic des Mémises (Walk 18)

39

View from the Refuge de la Dent d'Oche (Walk 20) photo Richard Saynor

plots and the total ascent have been extracted from the recorded GPS trails, after removing off-route wanders and smoothing GPS hiccups when too few satellites are available. GPS altitudes are accurate to about 10 metres at best, becoming tens of metres or worse in gorges or near steep cliffs.

Timings

The timings in this book are just an indication for a reasonably fit walker, and are mostly consistent with the times given on the local signposts. The actual times can be longer in bad weather, or when the slopes are slippery after recent rainfall; from bitter experience we also know they can increase significantly with age!

The timings do not include pauses for picnics, rests, taking photos or looking at flowers. It is important to leave an hour or so extra for this so as to enjoy your day.

SALEVE AND VUACHE

Geneva countryside and the Jura from the Salève (Walk 1)

The Salève and the Vuache are situated in the west of the Haute Savoie, to the south of Geneva. Both are limestone mountains that, geologically, belong to the Jura range and not to the Alps. Since they are lower than 1400m in altitude the walks here can be done early in the year, and you will meet numerous other walkers, some of whom are on the GR Balcon du Léman long-distance footpath which crosses this area.

Anyone who has been to Geneva has seen the Salève, for its long profile dominates the city, rising above the lake in front of the glistening snows of Mont Blanc. It has a long history, and tools and bones dating from

prehistoric times have been found in its caves. It has been part of the Savoie since the Middle Ages when one of the kings of Burgundy gifted land on its slopes to the church. In 1170 a Carthusian monastery was founded at Pomier near St-Blaise, whose guesthouse provided lodgings for the many pilgrims who passed through the area on their way to Santiago de Compostela in Spain.

The first exploration of the gorges and caves of the Salève was in the 18th century by the eminent Geneva scientist Horace Bénédict de Saussure, often considered the founder of alpinism. It was from its heights that he first saw Mont Blanc, which had not then been climbed, and offered a reward to the first person to climb it, going on to make the third ascent himself in 1787.

In the following century the beauty of the Salève was discovered by writers and poets of the Romantic Age, and then climbers started to find more and more difficult routes up its sheer cliffs. Once the Geneva section of the Swiss Alpine Club was founded in 1865, more routes were pioneered, one of which, the Grande Varappe, gave its name to the word for rock climbing in French, *varapper*. It was the club's members who secured the paths up the Grande Gorge and through the Grotte d'Orjobet, which is now one of the most exciting ways to approach the top of the mountain. The Salève also provided a training

ground for more prestigious expeditions, and some of the club's members were chosen for the Swiss expedition to Everest in 1952, paving the way for the first ascent by the British the following year.

Because of its proximity to Geneva the Salève is a very popular mountain, especially since it is accessible by road and cable car, one of the first to be built in 1894 and completely reconstructed 100 years later. In winter many come up for cross-country skiing, but by far the most popular activities are rock climbing and walking once the snow has disappeared.

Perhaps the loveliest walk on the Salève is along its grassy top, the Balcon du Salève, from where there

Geneva and the lake from the Balcon du Salève (Walk 2)

are magnificent views over Mont Blanc and the Alps on one side, and Geneva and its lake on the other. On a sunny day you will see numerous colourful paragliders taking off from the grassy slopes and drifting down to the plain below.

The Salève stretches for 19km, and there are some pretty little villages at the foot of its slopes, all with an interesting history – you might come across a monastery building, a wayside chapel or even a large château where you least expect it. There are a variety of walks from these, on paths that lead gently up through fields of grazing cows, past farms once owned by monks. The two highest points of the Salève, the Grand Piton and Pointe du Plan, can easily be reached from the villages of Beaumont and St-Blaise, and further south, near Cruseilles, is a walk on the other side of the mountain, starting from the attractive little lake at the leisure centre of Dronières.

The Vuache is a long, low ridge to the west of the Salève, its highest point being only 1100m. It is a continuation of the Jura range that, at its southwestern end, dips dramatically to let the River Rhône flow through a narrow defile called the Ecluse, guarded by a fort clinging to the rocky cliffs above. The Défilé de l'Ecluse is known locally as the Bellegarde Gap, and is visible from Geneva. The Vuache is on the far side of the Ecluse, and runs south for 14km to the village of Chaumont. It lies on a fault-line that creates occasional local earthquakes, the most recent being in 1996. Planes coming into Geneva from the north often fly over the mountain, and the motorway linking Geneva with Lyon tunnels beneath it.

Since this is the first mountain to be reached as you come up the Rhône valley from the warm south, it has a special microclimate attracting Mediterranean-type vegetation, and its flowers blossom well before others in the region. Many walkers come in early spring to see the rare dog's tooth violet and later on the carpets of alpine daffodils. The wooded ridge is home to several species of birds of prey, and the Défilé de l'Ecluse is on the migratory route for birds flying south. Nearby is the small town of Frangy, whose main claim to fame is the locally produced dry white wine called Roussette de Frangy.

The driving directions for walks in this section are from St-Julien-en-Genevois, near the Swiss border at Bardonnex to the southwest of Geneva. The town has an attractive centre, and there is plenty of accommodation available.

WALK 1
Gorges du Salève

Start/Finish	Le Coin, 665m
Distance	9km
Total ascent	690m
Grade	Medium
Time	4hr 15min
Maximum altitude	1295m
Map	IGN 3430 OT Mont Salève/St-Julien-en-Genevois/ Annemasse 1:25,000
Access	From St-Julien-en-Genevois, take the D1206 to Collonges and follow all signs to le Salève. At le Coin take the D45 towards le Salève/Croisette, and immediately after the turning leave your car in the large parking area on the right. In the car park there is an information board with a map of the walk.
Signposting	Good – new signposts, posts with yellow arrows on green, and red/white GR signs when on the Balcon du Léman
Note	Do not do this walk after it has been raining or snowing as the rocks can get very slippery and icy.

This is an exciting and dramatic walk up onto the Salève, the mountain which dominates Geneva. The limestone face is steep, making it a good training ground for rock climbers, and it was the Geneva section of the Swiss Alpine Club that created both paths used on this walk. The route up the mountain goes through the large and impressive Grotte d'Orjobet, and down through the Grande Gorge. Both paths are steep and protected in part by cables. As the Salève is within easy reach of Geneva all the walks on it are very popular, and you are likely to meet many other people, especially at weekends and at the top. There are magnificent views on the way up and down as well as on the summit, with Mont Blanc and the whole range of the Alps visible on one side, and the Geneva countryside and the Jura range of mountains on the other.

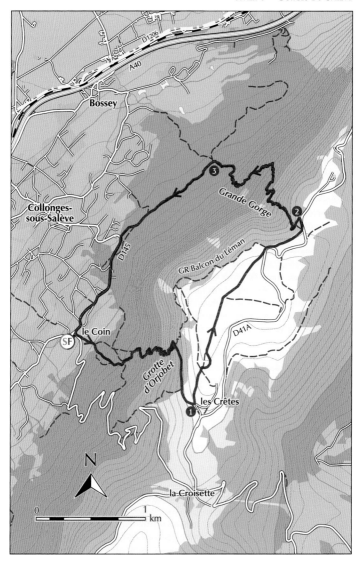

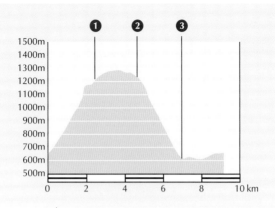

From the signpost at le Coin (665m), opposite the entrance to the car park, turn right and walk up the Chemin d'Orjobet towards Grotte d'Orjobet/Sur Orjobet. This is a narrow tarmac road that soon becomes stony, leading to a clearing on the left-hand side where there is the first of a series of information boards on the geology of the Salève.

Just after this you reach a fork where you go right, following the yellow arrow on the post. This is a steep track winding up through woods, clearly marked by posts with yellow arrows on green. The path becomes stony, going past a rock face. Continue upwards to reach the second information board (1hr 10min).

You then climb round an overhanging rock face on natural rocky steps with a metal barrier on the left and a cable for security on the right. Soon after you see the letters 'CAS 1905' painted in orange high above an opening in the rock face, which is the entrance to the **Grotte d'Orjobet**. ◄

Before entering the cave, go over to the viewpoint on the left, from where there is a dramatic view down over the Geneva countryside, with the Jura mountain range on the horizon.

At the entrance to the cave, beneath the orange letters, there is a small plaque on the wall saying 'Sentier d'Orjobet crée 1905 par la Section Genevoise du Club Alpin Suisse'. Walk past this to reach a long wooden plank with steps that you walk up to enter the cave.

Inside there are large steps cut out of the natural stone, with another metal cable. It takes about 10mins to climb up these through the cave and out on to the other side. Inside the cave there is a third information board, and a plaque erected in 2012 giving the history of the path through the cave.

> The **Grotte d'Orjobet** was first explored in 1779 by the eminent Geneva scientist H B de Saussure, who named it after his guide, François Orjobet, a native of le Coin. In 1905 the Geneva section of

At the entrance to the Grotte d'Orjobet

the Swiss Alpine Club created the path through the cave and were responsible for its upkeep until 2005, when it was handed over to the Association of the Salève, who upgraded the path between 2010 and 2012.

When you come out of the cave the path bears round to the right, curving round the side of the mountain to reach the GR Balcon du Léman at a T-junction and sign-post 'Sur Orjobet – alt. 1200m' (1hr 45min).

Walking up the fixed cables: photo Mike Goodyer

Go right, following the sign to la Bouillette/la Croisette. ▶ The path levels out somewhat and then comes out of the woodland onto the shoulder of the mountain.

Walk up the grassy slope to a reach a stile just before the road at a corner ❶. Do not go onto the road but turn hard left, leaving the GR, and follow the wide green path all along the top, with the lake down below on your left. On the right there is an aerial and a flag, indicating a jumping-off area for paragliders.

This is the ideal **picnic spot**. There are wonderful sweeping views of the Geneva countryside and the Jura range to the left, with the Alps to the right, dominated by Mont Blanc and the Dents du Midi, with the Môle in the foreground.

Follow the grassy track across pastures to reach the signpost 'Alpage des Crêts – alt. 1300m' (2hr 10min).

Continue straight on towards Grange Tournier/ Téléphérique, towards the observatory tower you can see

Left is a more difficult route via the Trou de la Tine/ la Corraterie, marked escarpé, meaning steep and exposed.

Paragliding off the Salève

49

The Môle from the top of the Salève

in the distance. The track reaches the road at a stone balustrade and another signpost at Sur le Charrot (1280m). Here you rejoin the GR for another short stretch. Following signs to Sur Grande Gorge, walk down across a meadow to reach the road again and a signpost 'Sur la Grande Gorge – alt. 1245m' (2hr 20min). Continue towards Sous Grande Gorge/le Coin par Grande Gorge, and turn off left into the woods, leaving the GR on a narrow path which winds downwards ❷.

Soon after you reach a rock face to the left where there is a plaque saying 'Grande Gorge 1854 to 1954', with the words 'Section Genevoise CAS' scratched out. At first you curl round the mountain and then the path becomes steep and stony with cliffs on each side. In one place there are rough stone steps and a chain to hold on to, and further down an iron railing. The path actually goes down the side of the **Grande Gorge** and there is a viewpoint from where you get a magnificent view looking back up at the precipitous cliffs with trees on the summit. Another plaque, which says 'Sentier de la Grande Gorge', explains that the path has been maintained since 1868 by the Geneva section of the Swiss Alpine Club.

Continue down the steep path, which skirts the Grande Gorge for a short while, and then goes down more steeply, with steps and cables to help you on the more difficult parts. ▶ The path goes back down the side of the Grande Gorge and becomes less steep as you get lower. You cross a stony patch in the woods before reaching a junction at the signpost 'Sous Gde Gorge Sud' ❸ (3hr 35min).

Go left following signs to le Pérouzet/le Coin (straight ahead goes to Bossy). This is a flat path over a boggy area on wooden slats, following the contour of the hill, and is a welcome relief after the long, steep, stony descent. On the left is the steep rock face of the Salève looking even more dramatic from below. Keep straight for 10mins until you arrive at a jeep track at a post with a yellow arrow. Turn left to meet a wider jeep track coming in from the left and continue to meet the road at the signpost 'le Pérouzet – alt. 620m' (3hr 50min).

Turn left, with tennis courts down below, and walk up the road (Route de la Croisette) towards **le Coin**, passing the Nymphéa Club on the left and then the Campus Adventiste du Salève on the right. Walk between the houses and round the corner to get back to the car park (4hr 15min).

Take care as this can be very slippery after rain or snow.

WALK 2
Balcon du Salève

Start/Finish	La Croisette, 1175m
Distance	7km
Total ascent	170m
Grade	Easy
Time	2hr
Maximum altitude	1295m
Map	IGN 3430 OT Mont Salève/St-Julien-en-Genevois/ Annemasse 1:25,000
Access	From St-Julien-en-Genevois, take the D1206 to Collonges and follow all signs to le Salève. At le Coin take the D45 towards le Salève/Croisette. This is a steep uphill drive of about 4km with a number of hairpin bends. There is plenty of parking at la Croisette at the top.
Signposting	Good – new signposts, posts with yellow arrows on green and red/white GR signs when on the Balcon du Léman

This is an easy walk for all the family, including young children, and can be done at almost any time of the year. In early spring the top of the mountain is carpeted with small white and purple crocuses, followed later by a blaze of dandelions. The walk gives magnificent views of Geneva and the surrounding countryside on one side, and Mont Blanc and the whole range of the Alps on the other. It was this view that inspired the eminent 18th-century Genevan scientist H B de Saussure (1740–1799), often considered the founder of alpinism, to explore the Alps further and to offer a reward to the first man to climb Mont Blanc.

Facing the line of the Alps, turn left and follow the signs saying 'Télépherique 6km/Monnetier 11km'. Walk past the Auberge des Montagnards and bear right up a jeep track on the Route des Rochers de Faverge. This becomes a grassy track that runs parallel to the road and regains

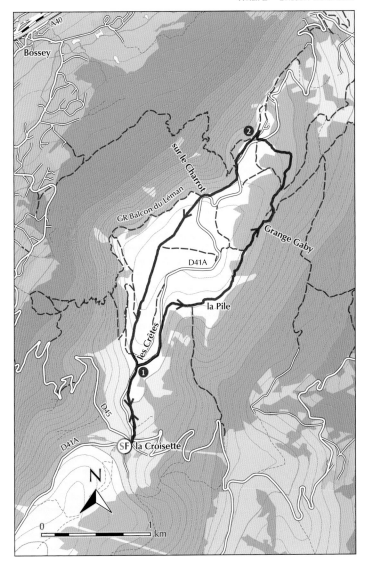

Bossey

A40

sur le Charrot

GR Balcon du Léman

Grange Gaby

D41A

la Pile

Les Crêtes

D45

D41A

SF la Croisette

N

0   1 km

53

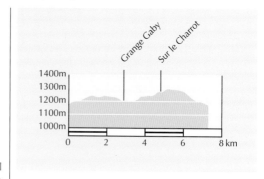

The road goes all the way along the top and you meet it again later on.

Angus Norton, Mike Woodman and Ben, walking along the Balcon du Salève

the road after 10mins at a signpost 'la Bouillette – alt. 1215m'. ◀

From here there are **spectacular views**. To the left is the town of Geneva with the Jura mountain range on the horizon. Behind is the Bellegarde Gap with the Fort de l'Ecluse on one side and the Vuache ridge on the other.

At the junction ❶ follow the main road, still the Route des Rochers de Faverge, to the right, signposted 'la Pile/Télépherique/la Muraz'. The TV aerial of **les Crêtes** is up on the left**.** After passing a wooden chalet on the left, look for a jeep track going down right and a signpost 'Sous les Crêtes – alt. 1220m', indicating that you are on the Balcon Paysager des Crêtes (20min).

The fenced jeep track initially loses height as it traverses round the mountain with the Alps on the right. You come to a large barn and house called **la Pile** (1230m). Follow the track in front of the farm buildings, which then becomes wide and grassy as it goes through an attractive old gnarled beech wood, passing two stagnant ponds, the second one in front of a newly renovated house called **Grange Gaby**. ▸

In the grounds here is a yurt advertised as 'Une yourte avec vue' which can be rented out overnight. It merits its name as the view from here is magnificent.

Turn right just before the gate of Grange Gaby and follow the yellow arrows down and round, skirting the house and pond. At a junction below the house keep left and follow the fence up to join the wide track again at the far end of the property. Turn right on the track and shortly after, at the signpost 'Grange Gaby – alt. 1210m', take the left track following the sign 'Balcon Paysager des Crêtes'. The track goes up gently through woodland and flattens out as it bears left. ▸ At a fork bear right to reach the D41A at an iron gate from where you can see the building of the television tower ahead (1hr).

There are carpets of white crocuses all along here in springtime.

This is the perfect place for a **picnic**, and there are several picnic tables. The view of the Alps and Mont Blanc from here must be the finest in the Geneva region, and if you detour up the road to the TV tower, there is a wonderful view over Geneva itself with the lake and the famous Jet d'Eau, and the Jura mountains beyond.

Cross the road to a signpost headed 'Observatoire' and go left towards Sur Grande Gorge/Grange Gaby/la Croisette to a gap in the fence ❷. Go through onto a grassy path, which goes left and back along the top of the Salève parallel to the D41A road. There are detours

Mont Blanc from the top of the Salève

to the right that are worth taking to get good views of the dramatic Grande Gorge, which dissects the north face of the mountain, and the lake and town of Geneva on the plain below. You are now on the long-distance Balcon du Léman for a short stretch.

After a few minutes you meet the road again briefly before bearing off to the right at a signpost 'Sur la Grande Gorge – alt. 1250m'. Follow signs to la Croisette and, still keeping near the road, go round the top of the Grande Gorge and continue straight to reach a stone balustrade and a signpost at **Sur le Charrot**, with more views over Geneva and the Jet d'Eau (1hr 20min).

Continue in the direction of Alpes des Crêtes/Panorama sur les Alpes/Croisette par les alpages. The grassy track goes across pastures through a fence and up, following a further fence on the left. Continue straight on at the signpost, making for a TV aerial and a windsock on the horizon ahead left. ◄ Keep straight through the fence at a green gate, past a fenced-off area for paragliders over on the right. As you draw parallel to the windsock, which is up on a hump to the left, the path forks right and descends to the road through a green gate at a hairpin bend. Continue straight down and a few minutes later you regain the D41A at ❶. Turn right and retrace your steps to **la Croisette** (2hr).

In springtime, watch for the many skylarks hovering in the air, recognisable by their melodious cry, streaked brown plumage, long wings and white-edged tails.

WALK 3
Grand Piton

Start/Finish	Beaumont, 750m
Distance	9.5km
Total ascent	630m
Grade	Medium
Time	3hr 45min
Maximum altitude	1380m
Map	IGN 3430 Mont Salève/St-Julien-en-Genevois/Annemasse 1:25,000
Access	From St-Julien-en-Genevois, take the D1201 towards Annecy/Cruseilles. After about 3km, turn left on the D177 to Beaumont. Go through the villages of les Chainays and Jussy to reach Beaumont (about 2km after the turn-off). Park your car behind the church where there is an information board entitled 'la Thuile/le Grand Piton' and a map of the walk. If you look upwards, you will see your destination, the Tour Bastian at the Grand Piton, on the skyline.
Signposting	Good – new signposts, posts with yellow arrows on green and red/white GR signs when on the Balcon du Léman

This is a fairly steep walk up to the Grand Piton, the highest point of the Salève. The tower at the top, known as the Tour Bastian, was built in 1820 by Claude Bastian who acquired the land on this side of the mountain from the Carthusian monastery of Pomier when it was sold off during the French Revolution. It was restored in 1983 by the commune of Beaumont and is frequently visited, as the views from it over the whole Geneva basin, with the Jura range behind, are magnificent.

Walk down to the Place de l'Eglise in front of the church where there is a statue of St Jacques de Compostelle,

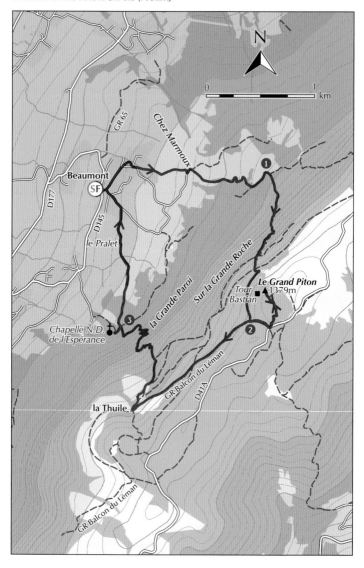

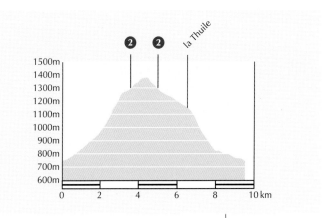

and cross over to the signpost opposite. ▶ Following the signs to le Grand Piton par les Travers, walk back up the road beside the church to the fork and go left up the Route des Pitons, towards les Travers/Chez Marmoux. (The Chemin de la Thuile to the right of the church, indicating les Pitons, is where you will come in on your return.) The road goes up through fields and new houses.

At the signpost 'les Travers – alt. 770m', just after an old stone cross on the right, take the road to the left (Chemin de Champ Côte) towards les Pitons. This goes to modern houses and then continues as a wide grassy track, going gently upwards to join a jeep track at a post with a yellow arrow on green. Turn right and shortly after you meet the road again. Branch left to a farm called **Chez Marmoux** where there is a stone fountain and, just after, a signpost (20min).

Following the sign indicating les Pitons, bear right at the side of the building and right again when the path forks (the signpost now says 'les Pitons 1hr 50min', whereas the previous one said 'les Pitons 1hr 40min'!). The path is broad and stony, going upwards through meadows, houses and woods towards another house, number 1600. Just before the entrance, take a path up to the right, indicated by a post with a yellow arrow. Keep

In the Middle Ages, one of the pilgrimage routes to visit the shrine of St James (St Jacques) in Santiago de Compostela passed through this area.

on the main path, following yellow arrows, to a fork with a signpost 'les Molliets – alt. 980m' ❶ (40min).

Go right towards le Grand Piton, and follow the posts with yellow arrows uphill. The path zigzags up through the woods following the contour of the hill, with a steep slope to the right. It becomes steep and rocky and, at a large faded red mark on a rock, curls left round a tall cliff face called **Sur la Grande Roche**. The path becomes steeper here and it is a bit of a scramble to get to the top of a rocky chimney. It then goes underneath a further cliff face, still on a rocky path, and continues upwards to cross a wide forest track at a small cairn. Go straight on a narrower ascending path through woods to reach a jeep track at a post. Cross over to reach a grassy track where you emerge onto the open hillside at a signpost 'Sous les Pitons – alt. 1250m' (1hr 35min).

Following the sign to la Thuile/les Pitons, go right on an attractive wide grassy track going round the contour of the hill, through tall coniferous trees and open glades. It reaches a water trough and marshy patch, due to a spring. Turn up left along a fence to the right and make for the two posts with yellow arrows you can see ahead. Turn right to go through the fence here, onto a narrow path that shortly reaches a T-junction and a signpost 'Sous les Pitons – alt. 1300m' ❷, where you join the red/white signs of the GR Balcon du Léman (1hr 55min). ◀

You will come back to this signpost on your return from le Grand Piton.

Follow the signs to les Pitons/le Grand Piton up to the left on a narrow track to reach the D41A road at a car park. Turn left and walk through the car park to a signpost 'les Pitons – alt. 1335m'. On a fine day in summer there will be lots of people here who come up by car and then make the short walk to the tower, but otherwise you will probably see nobody.

Follow the sign to le Grand Piton/Tour Bastian up the defined path through rocky glades and firs to a lovely open area. This is **Le Grand Piton**, at 1379m the highest point of the Salève, marked by the **Tour Bastian** standing on the very edge of the cliff (2hr 10min).

Le Grand Piton makes a lovely picnic spot, as you can sit on the edge of the cliff and look over the Geneva basin with the lake below in the foreground, and the Jura range behind. To the right are the cliffs leading round to the Grande Gorge. The poets Byron and Lamartine frequently visited this spot, and their names are engraved on a stone near the foot of the tower.

Retrace your steps to the car park and back down to the signpost 'Sous les Pitons – alt. 1300m' ❷. Turn left into the woods, following the signs to la Thuile/Beaumont par la Thuile. The path is well marked with red/white GR signs and yellow arrows on green. You come out of the woods into meadowland just above the attractive old farm of la Thuile, and shortly after you reach a jeep track at a signpost at **la Thuile** (1160m). Turn right and walk through the farm buildings, past an old round fountain dated 1893, to reach an information board about the farm (2hr 40min).

> The **Ferme de la Thuile** once belonged to the Carthusian monastery of Pomier, and was sold to Claude Bastian during the French Revolution. It was successfully farmed for many years by the Brand family, who invited visitors from Geneva up to participate in farming life, and was bought by the commune of Beaumont in 1982. It had fallen into disrepair, and by 2012 the once large fruit orchard, the highest in the Haute Savoie, contained only 12 trees. The commune is in the process of re-creating the orchard as it once was, and has planted 30 apple, pear, plum and cherry trees, all old and local varieties. There is a lovely view from the farm, over the entire Geneva basin and the Jura mountains.

The path goes past the front of the farm, to a signpost 'la Thuile – alt. 1156m'. Follow the signs to Chapelle N D de l'Espérance/Beaumont across a meadow to another signpost saying 'Route forestière de Beaumont' at the entrance to woods at a fork. Go left on a path, which zigzags down very steeply through woods. Follow the yellow arrows and keep on the main path, which goes straight over at two crossroads. There is quite a drop on one side and the path curls round just before you reach the high cliff of **la Grande Paroi** at a big rock fall on the right, to reach an intersection at a gravel road and a signpost 'Chapelle N.D de l'Espérance – alt. 840m' **❺** (3hr 15min).

> It takes just a few minutes to visit the attractive small stone chapel of **Notre Dame de l'Espérance**, built in 1985. Turn left and you come to a clearing with the chapel in front, with an image of the Virgin Mary on the outside. Inside are benches and

a large statue of Mary with a stained-glass window behind. Take a look at the visitors' book, which is full of rather touching messages. To the left of the clearing is an unusual crucifix. Jesus is made out of very modern black pincers and wire clippers, and the crown of thorns is a small piece of barbed wire – a really dramatic piece of artistry.

The modern chapel of Notre Dame de l'Espérance

Go back up to the previous signpost ❺ and take the gravel road indicating Beaumont église, following posts with yellow arrows. When it becomes paved, look to the right for a good view of the cliff face of la Grand Paroi and later the Tour Bastian on the Grand Piton. The road passes the houses of **le Pralet** and continues down to reach a main road at the signpost at Chemin de la Thuile. Turn left on the Chemin de la Grande Paroi to reach the church (3hr 45min).

WALK 4
Pointe du Plan

Start/Finish	Saint-Blaise, 880m
Distance	10km
Total ascent	590m
Grade	Medium
Time	4hr
Maximum altitude	1335m
Map	IGN 3430 OT Mont Salève/St-Julien-en-Genevois/ Annemasse 1:25,000
Access	From St-Julien-en-Genevois, take the D1201 towards Annecy/Cruseilles and at the hamlet of le Mont Sion, branch left at a signpost to Saint-Blaise on the D223. Continue 1.5km to the village and park in the car park opposite the church.
Signposting	Good – new signposts, some yellow arrows on green and red/white GR signs when on the Balcon du Léman and the GR65

This walk is partly in a nature reserve where chamois and roe deer can be found, as well as snowdrops, lilies of the valley, martagon lilies and lady's slipper orchids. It is a little known area of the Salève, where you will meet few other walkers except on the final stretch up to the Pointe itself, which is near a road. There are lovely sweeping views over Geneva on the way up and back, and a glorious view of Mont Blanc and the Alps from the Pointe.

> **Saint-Blaise** was first mentioned in 1029 when King Rudolph of Burgundy gifted the village, its inhabitants and the church, including all the land between 760m and 1188m, to the Abbey of Cluny. This was later acquired by Carthusian monks who built a monastery nearby at Pomier. They called the commune of Saint-Blaise 'Châtaigeraie' because of all the chestnut trees.

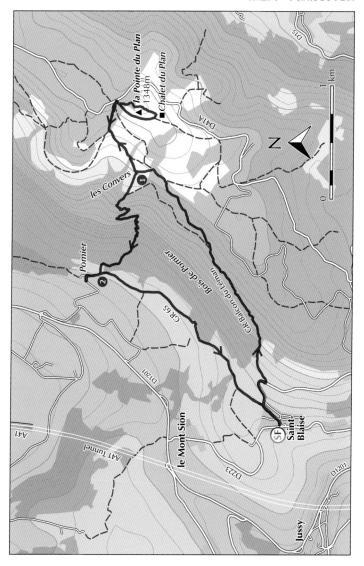

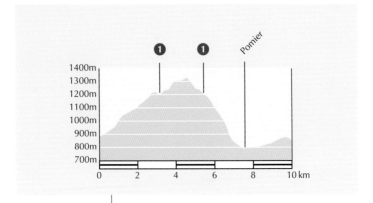

If you look back towards Saint-Blaise from here, you see the ridge of Le Vuache and the Plateau de Retord.

From the car park, cross the road to a signpost and walk up the Route du Salève towards Maison du Salève/ Chalets des Convers/le Grand Piton. A little way up on the left there is an information board with some history of Saint-Blaise and a panoramic map. ◄

Shortly after, at another signpost, you pass the small road on the left where you will emerge at the end of the walk. Continue up the road to the second bend where there is an old wooden sign on the left indicating 'Grand Piton 1hr 45min', and a new signpost indicating 'Grand Piton 2hr 05min'! (10min).

Go left up a sunken lane and after a few minutes the path branches to the left by a GR sign – both ways meet up further on. Follow the GR signs up a steep, rocky stre-ambed and at a T-junction bear left. After a lot of rain or snowmelt, this path can be very muddy. Continue steeply up following the GR signs and yellow arrows, ignoring all side turns. The path levels out for a while, undulating around the mountain through pleasant woodland called the **Bois de Pomier**, with attractive views over Geneva down to the left through breaks in the trees. Continue upwards to where the track comes out at the bottom of an open field.

Go through a gate and continue up the grassy slope to a signpost 'Sur les Convers – alt. 1220m'. Go left towards

Walking towards Convers farm

Chalet des Convers/Le Grand Piton through another gate and contour round to reach a fork. Following the GR signs, branch left down a sunken lane to reach the back of the dilapidated building of **les Convers** (1hr 10min). ▸

Go past a huge beech tree and the farm to a signpost at Chalet des Convers, which you will return to ❶. Follow the signs to Sous Plan du Salève/la Thuile/Grand Piton up the slope, with the fence on your left. This path takes you over a dry riverbed towards a stony jeep track at a hairpin bend and a signpost 'Sous Plan du Salève' (1hr 25min). Here you leave the GR markings. Just before you reach the jeep track, bear up right in a sort of wide grassy gully where there are no signs and no defined path. Ignore a path going off to the left and continue upwards to the top of the low ridge in front until you reach a fence on your left. The hump of the Pointe du Plan is up on the right. Follow the grassy track up to where it meets a tarmac road, the **D41A**, and a parking area.

Just before the car park, at the signpost headed 'les Torches', turn sharp right through an opening in the

This was originally the farm of the laybrothers (*convers*) of the Carthusian monastery of Pomier, which you visit later on the walk.

Mont Blanc and the Alps from Pointe du Plan

fence towards Pointe de vue du Plan, onto a jeep track. Continue towards another farm called **Chalet du Plan**, where there is a signpost. Turn left up the slope (there is no defined path) to reach the grassy hump of **la Pointe du Plan** (2hr).

> The **Pointe du Plan du Salève** has a stone trigonometric point on the top, and there is a glorious view right across the Alps, with Mont Blanc ahead, the Dents du Midi to the left, and Lac d'Annecy with its surrounding peaks to the right – an ideal picnic spot.

Go straight down the slope to the car park and retrace your steps down the grassy gully to the signpost at Sous Plan du Salève, and then turn left to reach les Convers farm and the signpost at ❶. Follow the signs to Pomier/ St-Blaise par Pomier on a faint path down the grassy slope to reach a fence where there is a yellow arrow and a stile, leading into woodland. ◄ At the start the path is wide but it narrows and becomes steep and stony after you pass a wooden hut with a picnic table on the left. It winds down

In the distance ahead you can see the Bellegarde Gap and the Fort de l'Ecluse, with the Jura mountains to the right.

through beech trees for about 20mins until you come to a stone cairn on the path and a yellow signpost pointing back up to les Convers (2hr 45min).

Turn left and continue down, passing another cairn. Keep going down this steep slope through the woods – you can see Pomier far beneath you. When you reach a T-junction turn left. The path widens as you continue down – keep on the main path and ignore others joining. You come to a clearing with a large rock in the centre marked 'le Rocher à Roger 2003'. Cross the clearing with the rock on your left and enter woodland again. ▶ Shortly after you pass a large cowshed on the right and reach the jeep track at the bottom of the slope and a T-junction at a signpost headed 'Pomier – alt. 800m' ❷ (3hr 15min).

Take a look here at the huge white cliff back to the right of where you have been clambering down – this is the southwestern end of the Salève.

It is worth taking a short detour to the right to have a look at **Pomier**. This a big old working farm with an attractive château-type house nearby, which used to be the main building of the Chartreuse de Pomier and is now used for conferences, concerts and banquets.

THE CHARTREUSE DE POMIER

Motto of the Carthusian order

This was a Carthusian monastery founded in 1170 by the followers of St Bruno (1030–1101). His first monastery was founded in 1084 in the mountains high above Grenoble, and all subsequent monasteries of this order were built in similarly isolated places. Fourteen monks lived at Pomier in individual 'cells' built around a large central cloister, each small building consisting of a workshop and wood store on the ground floor, with adjoining herb and vegetable garden, and a room upstairs for sleeping, eating and praying. The monks dedicated their lives to prayer, study and manual labour, and preserved a vow of silence, speaking to other monks only on a Sunday and having no contact with the outside world. Their food was grown and prepared by laybrothers (*convers*) who lived and farmed the land at les Convers. The laybrothers also dug a stream to provide water for the nearby mill, and constructed the road from Cruseilles to Geneva, replacing the old Roman road that went over the top of the Salève. The monastery was destroyed in 1793 at the time of the French Revolution, and the library was burned down. A series of arches is all that remains of the cloisters. It was rebuilt in 1894 as a hotel-restaurant and in 2001 was taken over by the present owners, who have erected a plaque on the outside wall with the motto of the Carthusian order: 'The Cross is steady while the world is turning'. Higher up the slope of the Salève there is a small grotto dug out of the rock face called l'Oratoire de St Bruno where there is an old wooden statue of St Bruno.

From ❷ follow signs left to Maison de Salève/Saint-Blaise/Col de Mont Sion, St Jacques de Compostelle. You are now on the **GR65** so look out for red/white markings.

In the Middle Ages 500–1000 **pilgrims** came through Pomier each year, on their way to visit the shrine of St James (St Jacques) in Santiago de Compostela in northeastern Spain. This route started in southern Germany, and passed through the Geneva area before continuing via le Puy. Many spent the night in the monastery guesthouse in Pomier before continuing on their journey, with another 1850km to go. Now the GR65 follows this route.

The track goes along the bottom of the hillside through scattered woods and open fields, and is a welcome relief after all the climbing you have done. You pass a wooden chalet on the right and join the old mule track to Saint-Blaise. After 30mins you come to the signpost at Sur les Fours and a T-junction. Continue straight on towards **Saint-Blaise**, and soon after you come out onto the D341. Turn right and in a few minutes you are back at the church (4hr).

WALK 5
Boucle de l'Iselet

Start/Finish	Lac des Dronières, Cruseilles, 785m
Distance	10.5km
Total ascent	345m
Grade	Easy
Time	3hr 15min
Maximum altitude	1130m
Map	IGN 3430 OT Mont Salève/St-Julien-en-Genevois/ Annemasse 1:25,000
Access	From St-Julien-en-Genevois, take the D1201 to Cruseilles, and at the roundabout at the entrance to the town take the D15 towards Roche sur Foron. After about 1km, at the junction of the D15 and D27, park on the right-hand side of the road by the roundabout, near the Lac des Dronières. At the parking area there is an information board entitled 'Clairière de l'Iselet' with a map of the walk, next to a signpost.
Signposting	Good – new signposts, some old wooden ones and plastic markers with yellow arrows on green

This is a gentle, easy walk on the western edge of the Salève, with glorious views of the Alps. It is a good winter walk when the snow is on the higher slopes, but it is also lovely in early springtime when the woodland flowers are in bloom.

The walk starts at the Lac des Dronières, an artificial lake built on wetland which originally belonged to the Carthusian monastery at Pomier. It has now been made into a major recreation centre, with a restaurant and picnic area, swimming pool, tennis courts, tree-top adventure course, fitness trail and deer park. The lake is a popular fishing site and a major breeding ground for frogs and toads, with 5000 arriving every spring to lay their eggs. The route ends by walking round the lake.

From the signpost at les Dronières (Parking) (790m), follow the signs to l'Abergement/l'Iselet and cross the two

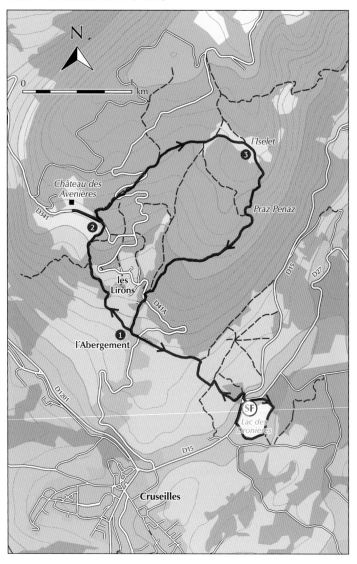

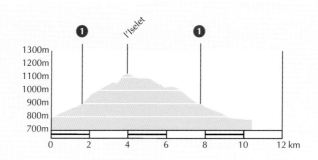

roads to reach a big stone cross opposite. Turn left onto a stony track to reach a post with a yellow arrow on green, and then turn left off the main track, following the yellow arrows up through the trees to reach a field. Bear right and continue up the side of the field to reach a junction and signpost headed 'les Biollays – alt. 825m' (10min).

Turn left, still following the signs to l'Abergement/ l'Iselet, on a stony jeep track which soon bears right

Autumn on the Salève

73

If you look back here, you will get a good view of the Dents du Midi on the left and, on the right, the Tournette and Parmelan mountains near Annecy.

between meadows to reach a T-junction. ◄ Turn left, following the post with yellow arrow, and keep on the main track. Continue through the houses of **l'Abergement** and keep straight on, crossing a small road and then the **D41A** to reach the centre of the village, Place du Bassin, where there is an old wooden signpost and a cross on a stone plinth. Following the signs to Circuit Avenieres/Iselet/Combe Isabelle, bear right on the Chemin du Creux and then left to reach a new signpost headed 'l'Abergement – alt. 880m' ❶ which you return to at the end of the walk (30min).

Go left towards l'Iselet on the Chemin Chez la Crimée, and follow this road for a few minutes until it leads onto a jeep track (yellow arrow on a tree). Keep right, ignoring tracks to the left, one saying 'Chemin Privé'. Then keep right again along a sunken bushy lane (do not go straight), which looks as though it might once have been an old mule track. There are lovely open fields down on the left, which give good views over the mountains, and up on the right is an old stone wall covered in brambles. The lane goes into fir and beech wood and then narrows as you slowly gain height. Be careful to follow the yellow arrows on green all along this wooded track as there are various forks. The track widens as it steadily gains height to reach the **D341**. Through the trees to the left you can see the **Château des Avenières** ❷ (1hr 5min). Turn left and walk along the road for a few minutes where you get a good view of the Alps and can see the château more closely.

The **Château des Avenières** was built by a rich American, Mary Wallace Shillito, between 1907 and 1913. Her Indian husband, Assan Farid Dina, designed the garden and built the chapel in 1917. He also did much for the Salève region, financing the provision of electricity and drinking water in the surrounding villages. His goal was to build an observatory on top of the Salève with the biggest telescope in the world, and although this was never realised, in 1925 he became the owner of the Vallot Observatory high on Mont Blanc. He died in 1928

*Château des
Avenières*

while on a cruise in the Red Sea, and his widow
Mary sold the château in 1936. She died two years
later, having had her fortune depleted by her second husband, a Swiss pianist. The château became
a rest home run by the Red Cross and then a school
until 1994 when, after considerable restoration, it
opened as a luxury hotel-restaurant.

Retrace your steps back to where you came onto the
road at ❷ and go left and then right, following the yellow
arrows. At a fork bear right and at the next fork bear left
(here there is a small stone marker with the letter S on
one side and G3 on the other). Shortly after you reach the
D41A on a hairpin bend. Go straight across and follow
the yellow VTT sign through the trees to reach the road
again. Go straight across to cut off another corner, and
when you get to the road cross over to reach a small parking area on the opposite side, next to a signpost headed
'Combe Isabelle – alt. 1080m' (1hr 30min).

Continue straight on towards l'Iselet on a wide jeep
track through coniferous woods. Follow the yellow arrows
on green until you reach an old wooden board saying
'Combe Isabelle'. Go through the gate into the Alpage
de l'Iselet, an attractive open area bordered by woodland
with some magnificent fir trees, and continue on a grassy

This is the highest point of the walk, and a good place to stop and have a picnic as there is a lovely view of the Alps.

track to the signpost at **l'Iselet** (this is broken on one side). Continue straight on to reach an isolated farm on the left, the Chalet du Lislet, set in a sort of dip in the hills, with three gigantic lime trees beside it (1hr 45min). ◄

Go through a gate in the fence (VTT sign) and bear up right across open meadowland to a new signpost 'Chalet de l'Iselet – alt. 1120m'. Follow the sign to l'Abergement and bear right on a track down through woods ❸, with a fence on your right for part of the way. It takes you through a clearing and briefly into the woods again before reaching a larger clearing and signpost headed **Pré Penaz** (Praz Penaz on the map) (1090m). Again follow the sign to l'Abergement down to the start of a large field (yellow arrow on a tree). As you walk down the side of the field, you can see a heap of stones over on the left, which is all that remains of the farm that was once here, with a lovely view overlooking the Alps. At the bottom of the field bear right on what used to be the track to the farm and continue past an overgrown pond on the right.

Just beyond the pond bear left at a post with a yellow arrow and go through a gate to reach a signpost saying '3 Est Abergement'. Stay on the sunken main track downwards through beech woods to reach a T-junction. Turn left and follow the yellow arrows down to the road (2hr 30min).

Turn left and almost immediately, at an unmarked post just after a hairpin bend and road railings, turn right down a path. Continue down until you meet a road again (the village of les Lirons is up to the right) and then bear left. You will soon be on the outskirts of l'Abergement and you pass, to the right, the road you took on the outward journey and come to the signpost 'l'Abergement – alt. 880m' at ❶.

Go straight on towards les Dronières (Parking), and at the stone cross in the village centre, bear left. Continue straight on at the crossroads, on the Rue du Mont Blanc, and follow the yellow arrows on green back to the parking, on the way you came up (3hr). Turn left at the information board and go through the barrier down to the lake and walk around it (3hr 15min).

WALK 6
Le Vuache

Start/Finish	Chaumont, 595m
Distance	7.5km
Total ascent	520m
Grade	Easy
Time	3hr
Maximum altitude	1110m
Map	IGN 3330 OT Bellegarde-sur-Valserine 1:25,000
Access	From St-Julien-en-Genevois, take the D1206 towards Bellegarde and after 5km, at the village of Viry, turn left onto the D992 towards Frangy. Continue on this road for about 12km and, just after le Malpas, take the right fork to Chaumont on the D147. There are parking places just before the church on the left, at the side of the road on the right and behind the Auberge de Pralet, a good place for a drink or a meal after your walk.
Signposting	Good – new signposts, rectangles with yellow arrows on green and red/white GR signs for the Balcon du Léman

This is a popular springtime walk for all flower lovers, and for many it is a yearly ritual to see the carpets of flowers, especially the rare dog's tooth violet. The best time to go is in late March or early April when the first spring sun warms the slopes, and then a little later when the alpine daffodils take over. The plants here are all protected, and you will see signs asking you not to pick the flowers or the holly, nor to dig up the bulbs.

The village of **Chaumont** is strategically situated between the Vuache ridge and Mont Chauve, and on the hill above are the ruins of a 12th-century castle. Chaumont used to be a small bustling commercial centre with its own market, but fell into decline in the 17th century; now it is coming back to life, and many houses are being restored. The church is worth a visit if it is open as it has some attractive stained-glass windows.

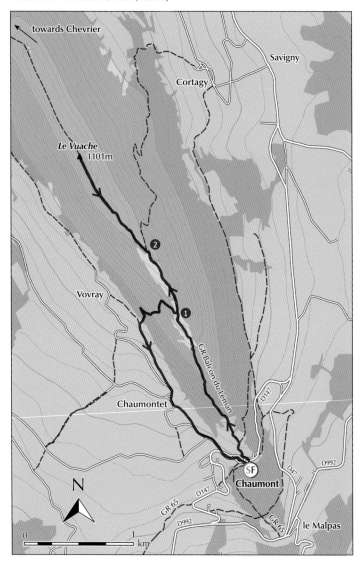

towards Chevrier

Savigny

Cortagy

Le Vuache
1101m

2

Vovray

1

GR Balcon du Léman

Chaumontet

Chaumont

D147

D147

D47

D992

D992

N

0   1
                        km

GR 65

D992

GR 65

le Malpas

SF
Chaumont

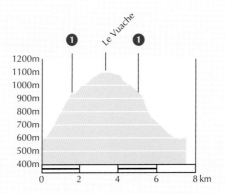

Walk behind the church and bear left to reach a new signpost at the foot of the Impasse de Vuache on the right. Following signs for Sommet du Vuache, go up this stony lane, which has a crumbling wall covered with ivy on the right. ▶ At a sign indicating le Mont (630m), continue straight through two gates – do not take the track on the right towards Vuache par Cortagy. The path is steep and stony, and clearly marked with yellow arrows on green and red/white signs for the **GR Balcon du Léman**. After about 20mins you come to a large information board on the left.

In spring the banks are covered with blue periwinkle, primroses and both blue and white violets.

> The information board summarises the **flowers and fault lines** associated with the Vuache. One side is entitled 'Flore et Faune Méridionales', and has illustrations of the flowers that flourish on the sunny south-facing slopes. The other is entitled 'La Grande Faille du Vuache', and has maps and explanations of the fault-line which runs under the Vuache and which has resulted in several minor earthquakes since 1332, the most recent being in 1996.

The path comes out of the woods as you pass under the wires of a pylon. You are now on the open slope of the mountain with an uninterrupted view down the Usses valley with the Jura mountains on the other side.

FLOWERS ON THE VUACHE

Dog's tooth violets on the Vuache

In early spring the grassy slopes are covered with delicate blue scillas (*scilla bifolia*) and yellow gageas (*gagea lutea*), and in the woods there are hundreds of dog's tooth violets (*erythronium dens-canis*). These are not violets at all but belong to the lily family, with a white bulb somewhat like a dog's tooth and distinctive mottled leaves. The flowers are a striking pink with narrow petals pointing backwards and prominent stamens. Higher up in the woods are delicate white snowflakes (*leucojum vernum*), their nodding bells tipped with yellow, and pink corydalis. The alpine daffodils (*narcissus pseudonarcissus*) come out later, making brilliant patches of yellow under the trees higher up. If you do the walk in early summer, the woods will be full of rampions (*allium ursinum*) with their strong garlic smell, and you will see some of the flowers which were illustrated on the noticeboard lower down, including the beautiful purplish pink martagon lilies (*lilium martagon*) and several species of orchids.

This is the path you will take on the return leg.

At the signpost 'Sur la Montagne – alt. 930m' ❶, the post points left to Vovray (1hr 5min). ◄ Continue straight on towards Sommet du Vuache, past a newly built wall to the right. Here there are several holly bushes, with signs further on asking you not to pick the holly. Almost immediately you are in open grassland again for a short time.

As you go back into woodland, ignore a wider track going down to the right ❷ and follow the yellow arrow and GR sign straight on, past two information boards on the flowers and wildlife of the Vuache. The path bears to the left and winds up a rocky bluff to reach a viewpoint (1hr 20min).

From this **viewpoint** you get sweeping views on both sides – to the right the Usses valley and Jura again, and to the left the city of Geneva with the Jet d'Eau rising above the lake. In the distance there is a glistening row of snow-covered peaks, dominated by Mont Blanc. This makes a good picnic spot.

The track bears to the right at a yellow arrow and GR sign, and you are now on the ridge proper. This is a well-trodden path which flattens as it winds through beech woods, passing a few concrete boundary markers. ▶ The path continues for about 20mins, and on the left are a few places where you can walk to the grassy edge and look down onto the motorway which tunnels right under the Vuache. You finally come to a large cairn and a wooden sign at **Le Vuache** (1101m), which is the highest point of the ridge (1hr 40min).

In early March look out for white snowflake flowers under the trees, and later for masses of alpine daffodils.

The **GR Balcon du Léman** continues to Chevrier at the northern end of Le Vuache, on its way round the mountain crests on the French side of Lake Geneva (Lac Léman). It then turns northeast, skirting the city of Geneva, and follows the crests of the Jura – the Grand Crêt d'Eau, Reculet, Crêt de la Neige and Colomby de Gex. The last short stretch is in Switzerland, culminating just beyond the summit of the Dôle, above the town of Nyon.

The Balcon du Léman arrives at Chaumont, at the southern end of Le Vuache, from the east, having traversed a string of peaks along the south of Lake Geneva, starting at St-Gingolph on the French-Swiss border, at the foot of the Dent d'Oche, and continuing through the Pré-Alpes, into the Vallée Verte, and across the length of the Salève.

From the cairn retrace your steps to the signpost at Sur la Montagne ❶ (2hr 10min). Leaving the GR, follow the signs to Vovray down across the meadow to reach woodland again at a wooden sign indicating Chaumont par Vovray and a yellow arrow on green. Go through

Walking down to Chaumont

the fence and continue to the right along the path. This becomes fairly steep as it winds down through woods where there are more dog's tooth violets and daffodils in springtime. You eventually come out of the woods into a field where there is a small chalet up on the right, with the summit of the Vuache visible behind it. Cross the field to a jeep track and signpost 'Champs Rosset – alt. 730m' (2hr 40min).

Turn left towards Chaumont, and then at the yellow arrow go straight on through trees and fields for about 10mins until you meet the tarmac road in the pretty hamlet of **Chaumontet**. ◄ Bear left and left again at a T-junction where there is a large cross and a yellow arrow. At the first bend, at a yellow arrow just before a wooden chalet, take the Chemin des Voiries to the left. Here there is a lovely view of Chaumont and beyond is the sharp outline of the Parmelan and La Tournette near Annecy, with the snow-covered Alps in the background. The path reaches the road at a cross where you turn left, past the cemetery, and follow the road into **Chaumont** (3hr).

Grapes for the local white wine, Roussette de Frangy, are grown here, and you pass a farm where the wine is made.

VALLÉE VERTE

The Vallée Verte and Lake Geneva from the Montagne d'Hirmentaz (Walk 10)

The Vallée Verte follows the River Menoge from where it flows into the Arve near Annemasse up to its source near Thonon-les-Bains. This beautiful, green valley lives up to its name, and is an area of rich agricultural land and low rolling hills which has remained remarkably unspoilt, despite its proximity to Geneva. The small villages are each centred round an attractive church, for this has been a deeply Catholic area since the reconversion by St François de Sales after the Reformation, and you will find many chapels, wayside shrines and crucifixes, as well as Stations of the Cross and statues on mountain tops, a custom fashionable in the 18th and 19th centuries. As the mountains are not high here, none of the walks in this section are difficult, yet all give spectacular views to the north across Lake Geneva and south to Mont Blanc. The GR Balcon du Léman continues through this area.

Entering the valley from Annemasse in the west, you first come to the long Voirons ridge, another landmark visible from the lakeside at Geneva. The ridge was once owned by the Counts of Boëge who built a castle and chapel on its heights, and

Mont Forchat and the Vallée Verte (Walk 11)

in the 20th century a secluded monastery was built, which has become a centre of spiritual healing. The Voirons is now a nature reserve where animals are protected, and there is a lovely walk along the top of the ridge which gives magnificent views for its entire length.

At the southern end of the River Menoge is the low Mont de Vouan, another area of historical interest. From the time of the Romans to the start of the 20th century, stone was quarried here to make millstones, and impressions of these can still be seen in the quarries on the way up the mountain.

Further up the River Menoge is the small town of Boëge, the *chef-lieu* (capital) of the region and a good base for walks in the Vallée Verte. The square next to the church has an old covered market hall where a weekly market takes place. A little further north is the town of Villard, in the centre of attractive farmland, where the sides of many of the old farms are still made of fir-wood squares called *tavaillons*. The walk up to the Pointe de Miribel starts here, and you can follow the Stations of the Cross up to the statue of the Virgin Mary on the summit, as countless worshippers have done in the past.

The highest village in the valley is Habère-Poche, a centre for both cross-country and downhill skiing at the foot of the Montagne d'Hirmentaz. Despite the ski installations on the far side of the ridge, this makes a lovely walk with spectacular views for you are now nearer to Lake Geneva. Near the source of the Menoge is the walk up Mont Forchat, another peak with a statue on its summit, this time of the locally revered St François de Sales.

The driving directions for walks in this section are from Boëge or further down the valley.

WALK 7
Signal des Voirons

Start/Finish	Le Penaz, near Boëge, 820m
Distance	12km
Total ascent	785m
Grade	Medium
Time	4hr 45min
Maximum altitude	1475m
Map	IGN 3429 ET Bonneville/Cluses 1:25,000
Access	From Boëge, take the D20 towards Saxel. Just after the Boëge end-of-village sign, turn left on the Route de Perriers and follow this road round to the left where it says Auberge du Chalet (if you go straight you end up in a farmyard). Keep left at the next junction and then bear up right following the signs to Penaz (about 2km from Boëge). Drive up until you see a small parking area on the right with an information board entitled 'Au Pied des Voirons'.
Signposting	Good as far as la Moutonnière with new signposts and posts with yellow arrows on green. There are some faded white splashes up to the monastery and then red/white GR signs for the Balcon du Léman. After la Moutonnière the route finding is not easy as there are only old wooden signposts, which are difficult to read, a few faded white splashes and red/yellow markings for the short distance of the GRP Tour de la Vallée Verte.

The Voirons ridge is clearly visible from the lakeshore at Geneva, and this is a popular walk, especially in the summer months. After a fairly steep ascent through the trees there is a gentle, undulating path along the ridge, with spectacular views of Mont Blanc and the Alps. The Voirons is a nature reserve where red deer, roe deer, wild boar and even the rare lynx are to be found.

The walk has a lot of historical interest as the ridge has been a holy site since prehistoric times. In the Middle Ages the land was owned by the counts of Boëge, who built a castle guarding the valley and a chapel on the heights. The 20th-century Monastère de Bethléem is a well-known centre of pilgrimage and spiritual healing.

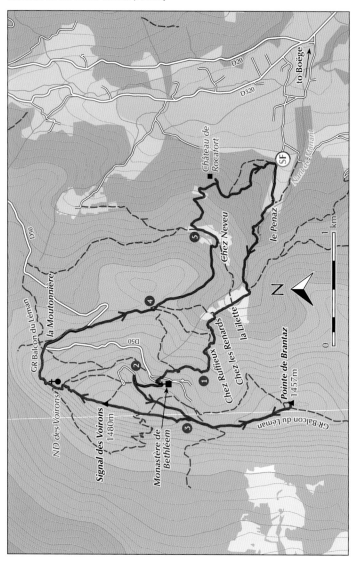

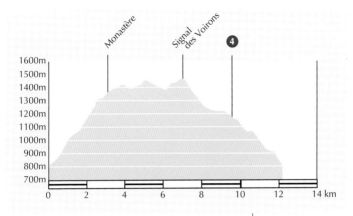

Walk up the road to the houses of le Penaz and look for a signpost at the rear of the top house on the right. Follow the signs to la Lilette/le Monastère/Signal des Voirons up a wide wooded path, with periwinkles flowering on the banks in springtime. Down on the left there is a narrow stream, the **Nant de Manant**, and the sound of rushing water is delightful company for the first part of your walk upwards through woodland. At an obvious fork go right, although it is worth taking a short detour to the left to see a lovely waterfall. This is a steep path through mixed woodland, initially under electricity cables, with water cascading down the rocks on your left. The track bears to the left to cross a stone bridge where another stream comes down from the right to join the original one, which is still beside you on the left, level with the path (40min).

At a yellow arrow on green the path meets a jeep track and signpost at la Lilette (1079m). Turn right to le Monastère/Signal des Voirons (left indicates Sur les Côtes/la Molière). This is where the Tour de la Vallée Verte (red/yellow signs) joins briefly before going off right to Chez Neveu. Shortly after you come to a large grassy clearing where there is a recently restored farm called **la Lilette**, and another signpost. Keep straight on following the signs to Monastère/Signal des Voirons up to **Chez les Renards**,

The farm buildings of Chez les Renards

another farm and house with various outbuildings. At the signpost turn left to Monastère and then almost immediately go round behind a house (do not go straight on). The path climbs up fairly steeply and joins a jeep track at a sign at **Chez Ruffieux** (1211m) (1hr 10min).

At the signpost turn left towards Monastère, passing an old house with a small modern statue of the Virgin Mary high on the outer wall and a ruin on the right – this was originally a priest's house. ◀ Immediately after the house bear to the right at a fork (the main path continues straight). There are several paths here, so look carefully for faded white splashes on trees (note that a white cross indicates the wrong way). The path goes upwards through dense coniferous forest and becomes narrow and sunken. At a wooden signpost indicating Monastère/le Signal, where there is a red/white flash on a tree, the path goes sharply back to the right ❶.

Just after this bend you will come to the high green wire fence surrounding the monastery and a wooden gate, from where you can see the monastery buildings above you. ◀ The narrow path contours round to the right, going slightly uphill, with the fence and monastery

Look back here for a magnificent view of Mont Blanc and the valley below.

Do not attempt to get into the monastery grounds as it is private property.

grounds on the left. The path forks at the signpost indicating 'Parking du Monastère', and you go up to the left. Keep alongside the fence, crossing a small gully, where the fence turns up to the left. The trees are dense here, and if there has been recent logging you may have to negotiate fallen trees or branches. Look carefully for faded white markings. Continue round to the right, contouring along below the monastery buildings to reach another wooden signpost with a GR sign indicating Monastère/le Signal. The path soon starts to go up, with wooden steps leading to the outer buildings of the monastery on the left, with the church and shop. Continue up to the road and car park to the right (1hr 35min).

The **Monastère de Bethléem** was built in the 1980s for the Sisters of Bethlehem, and now there are 100 nuns living here. Following the rule of St Bruno, founder of the Carthusian Order, the nuns have dedicated their lives to prayer, poverty and manual work. They live in silence and solitude, in

Monastère de Bethléem from the Voirons ridge

individual chalets, cut off from the outer world and for much of the time from each other. It is possible to stay here on retreats, in order to spend a period of time in silent worship, but otherwise you cannot enter the monastery. Outside the monastery there is a sanctuary that is open to visitors, and a shop selling pottery and other religious goods made by the nuns. This is open most afternoons, except Sundays.

It is possible at this point to take a direct route to the Signal des Voirons, shortening the walk by about 50mins, but you would miss the lovely walk along the ridge.

Cross the road with the car park on your right and follow the narrow path going straight up, signposted 'Signal des Voirons 25min/Pointe de Brantaz 45min'. Follow the signs which take a short cut to meet the road again and turn right, rounding a corner. Stay on the road for about 5mins, then at the next bend turn hard left at a signpost towards Piste de la Transfiguration/Crêtes de Voirons/Pointe de Brantaz ❷. ◄

Follow the wide, flattish track, which reaches a yellow arrow on green by a sign entitled 'Massif des Voirons Site Protégé' ❸. Look out for this waymark, as you will come past here on your return along the ridge. Go left onto the **GR Balcon du Léman**, which you follow as far as the Pointe de Brantaz and then back to the Signal des Voirons and Moutonnière, so watch for red/white markings. Keep going as the track starts to descend and reaches the Col de Prieuré, 1392m. It flattens as it goes along the ridge through woods, then goes gradually up to reach the **Pointe de Brantaz** at a signpost. Turn left for about 100 metres and walk up to the panorama viewpoint at 1457m (2hr 15min).

From the **Pointe de Brantaz** there are lovely views into the valley below, with the Mont Blanc massif and the Dents du Midi on the skyline. This is a good place to have a rest and is less crowded in summer than the Signal des Voirons itself.

You can clearly see the monastery buildings below, with the individual chalets where each nun lives in solitude.

Retrace your steps and turn right to walk back along the ridge on the same path. ◄ Just after the Col du Prieuré look out for the yellow arrow on green and the 'Massif des Voirons Site Protégé' sign which you passed on the way along the ridge ❺. Follow the yellow arrow up a narrow sandy path on the left which bears right and climbs up to take you right along the ridge. You reach a bench and a viewpoint at the Saut de la Pucelle (1430m), overlooking the Geneva countryside and the lake, with the Salève and the Môle behind you.

> The legend behind the name **Saut de la Pucelle** ('the virgin's leap') goes back to the Middle Ages when a beautiful young girl lived on the mountain with her parents. The falconer of the Count of Boëge fell in love with her, but she rejected his advances. One day she was sitting up here all alone when he approached her. Preferring death to dishonour, she threw herself off the steep cliff.

Continue on the ridge track until, just before the Signal des Voirons, you reach a signpost where a path on the right comes up from the monastery. At the **Signal des Voirons** (1480m), there is an IGN stone survey marker dated 1958, and a lovely view of Mont Blanc and the Dents du Midi (2hr 45min).

Go straight on towards Prieuré Notre Dame des Voirons/Granges Gaillard, still following the red/white GR signs. The path winds downwards for 15mins, sometimes quite steeply through bushes. Keep looking for the signs as sometimes the track is not well defined. Just before you arrive at the chapel of **ND des Voirons**, which is 100m lower than the Signal, there is a steep and rocky section to scramble down (3hr).

NOTRE DAME DES VOIRONS

The old chapel of Notre Dame is in a grassy clearing by a large old house. On the chapel there is this inscription (translated): 'The chapel, dedicated to the Virgin Mary, has been a place of pilgrimage for five centuries. People have come here with their burdens and through their prayers have received grace and benediction.'

The first chapel was erected in 1456 by Louis de Langin, who owned most of the land on the mountain. When out hunting one day Louis was attacked by a wild boar and in desperation he prayed to the Virgin Mary to save him, promising to build a chapel in her honour if she did so. He survived his injuries and, together with a small band of followers, spent the rest of his life in prayer and thanksgiving at the small monastery he built here. Inside the chapel was a beautiful statue of the Virgin sculpted in black Lebanese cedar, which performed many miracles. The original buildings were burnt down and rebuilt several times, and in 1852 the black statue of the Virgin Mary was brought down from the mountain and placed in the newly constructed parish church in Boëge.

Walk down in front of the church, past the entrance on the left, to a post with a yellow arrow and a red/white sign. Go down the wooden steps, bearing right. You are still on the Balcon du Léman, so follow red/white signs and posts with yellow arrows. This is initially a narrow path which starts to descend through a young fir plantation. ◄ Continue past a signpost 'Notre Dame dessous – alt. 1360m', towards la Moutonnière. The path meets a wider track where you turn down to the right, continuing down through more mature fir trees to reach a hairpin bend at **la Moutonnière**, on the tarmac road leading to the monastery (3hr 15min). Here you leave the Balcon du Léman and the red/white markings.

There are lovely views of the lake and Jura mountains beyond on the left.

Walk down the road for about 10mins and look for a wide jeep track off to the right. About 20 metres along this track look carefully for an old wooden sign on the right indicating 'Monastère/Près du Tayes/Pointe de Brantaz' – this is not obvious. Go along this muddy, flattish track until you come to a wide clearing which is Près du Tayes ❹. Cross the clearing to where there is an old cabin and a picnic table, and take the jeep track furthest to the left, by a wooden sign indicating Chez Neveu (3hr 35min). There are four tracks going off here, so be careful not to take the one back to Chez les Renards or up to the monastery.

Go down the wide jeep track, through mixed beech and fir woods, until you reach a house on your right called 'le Renardière'. Soon you come to an attractive clearing.

Follow the obvious path through the clearing and after some trees, you see the farm buildings of **Chez Neveu** ahead. Do not go down to the farm, but as you come out of the trees, look carefully for an old wooden signpost on the right. Turn left towards Saxel (right goes to St André). The track goes across the top of the meadow, following faded red/yellow markings of the GRP Tour de la Vallée Verte which you briefly join. Below you are some gnarled old fruit trees. Shortly after you reach an old wooden signpost pointing back to le Monastère ❺. This is where you leave the red/yellow markings (4hr 15min).

▸ Immediately at the signpost, look for an old wooden arrow on the first tree to the right (this is almost impossible to see). Turn right here into the woods on a barely obvious path, with some faded white splashes. As the path rounds a small hill it becomes more defined, and there are more lovely views of the Vallée Verte and Mont Blanc. The path winds down to reach a picnic table and an information board on the Boucle de Rocafort and the 'Copacou'.

> You need to be very careful here as the next turning is not at all obvious.

> The **Copacou** is a cupule or cup stone, used for sacrifice. These stones were generally found on high ground, and are thought to date back to prehistoric

Information board at the Copacou stone

times. The victim's head was pushed back into a shallow cuplike depression, and then his throat was cut so that the blood flowed down the steep side of the rock.

The track turns to the left here and goes down fairly steeply through another area denuded of trees to reach a jeep track at the bottom of the hill. You can see the remains of **Château de Rocafort** on your left, which is worth a short detour.

The old **castle of Rocafort** was built in the 12th century by one of the counts of Boëge, on a site fortified by the Romans. It is strategically situated on the east side of the Voirons ridge and dominated the valley from Boëge to the Col de Saxel. It suffered numerous sieges, mainly from the Dukes of Savoy, and was finally abandoned in the 14th century. The ruins are in the process of being restored, and one day the castle will doubtless be opened to the public.

After visiting the castle, turn right to le Penaz on a wide path through woodland, hugging the contour of the hill. Keep on this path following white splashes until you come to a track going steeply down left.

There is an information board about **millstones** on right side of the main path, just above where your track turns off, explaining their uses and how they are quarried. Millstones were used for grinding corn, pressing apples for cider and also for sharpening knives. Just above this board there is a finished millstone, and the outline of an unfinished one carved in the rock. The Vallée Verte was famous for its millstone quarries, two of which can be visited on Walk 8, Mont de Vouan, and a description of how the stones were made is at the beginning of that walk.

Follow the track down until you reach the car park at **le Penaz** (4hr 45min).

WALK 8

Mont de Vouan

Start/Finish	Boisinges, near Viuz-en-Sallaz, 630m
Distance	8km
Total ascent	455m
Grade	Medium
Time	3hr 15min
Maximum altitude	965m
Map	IGN 3429 ET Bonneville/Cluses 1:25,000
Access	From Viuz-en-Sallaz, take the D907 towards Pont de Fillinges and turn right onto the D190 through Boisinges. Continue straight on the D292 to reach a grassy triangle and parking area saying 'Bourguignons Parking – alt. 630m', with a notice board entitled 'Meulières de Vouan'. Drive along the wide jeep track on the left and turn right at a T-junction on the Route de Vouan (the signpost indicates les Sellières) to the water spout called la Source qui Rit. Continue a few metres to a small parking area at another notice board entitled 'Meulières de Vouan' and a signpost 'la Source qui Rit (Parking) – alt. 610m'.
Signposting	Mostly good except for one section – new signposts and old wooden ones, some posts with yellow arrows on green

This is an easy walk for much of the way, although part of the descent can be tricky. As it is not high it is a good walk at any time of the year, even in winter when the lovely views from the ridge are perhaps better with no leaves on the trees. It is also well worth doing for its historical value as it includes a visit to two ancient millstone quarries (*meulières*).

From the parking area at la Source qui Rit, follow the sign 'la Gouille au Morts/Meulières à Vachat/Crêtes de Vouan' and walk along the jeep track, which gets stonier. On the right are the exposed rocky cliffs of the tree-covered Vouan ridge. At the first signpost 'Ru du Trou des Fées – alt. 650m', continue straight on, still towards la Gouille

QUARRYING MILLSTONES

An old millstone

The area around Mont de Vouan, which is situated at the entrance of the Vallée Verte, was used for quarrying stones from Roman times to the start of the 20th century. Over the centuries 100,000 millstones and fruit presses were hewn out of these quarries – a very lucrative business, as one millstone was worth the price of a house. In order to make a millstone, the workers chipped out a perfect circle in the rock face which they then filled up with wood. The wood was watered till it swelled and forced the stone away from the rock face. The enormously heavy circles of rock were then hauled down the sides of the mountain by means of ropes and pulleys – an amazing and exhausting feat of endurance.

As well as the fascinating impressions of the millstones left in the rock face at two sites on the walk, there are innumerable shell fossils from the time when this area was under the sea thousands of years ago.

If you have the time, pay a visit to the Musée Paysan in Viuz-en-Sallaz, which will give you a fascinating insight into the lives of the people in the region up to the last century. Check the website for opening hours www. paysalp.fr.

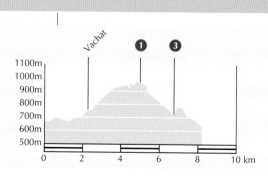

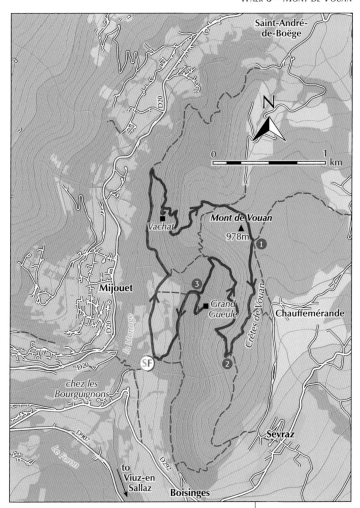

au Morts/Meulières à Vachat/Crêtes de Vouan. At a further sign headed 'Ru du 1er Trou' in a clearing, go left towards la Gouille au Morts and continue along through a patch of fir trees. Later you pass a delightful marshy area with a pond.

> **La Source qui Rit**, which means 'laughing fountain', is merely an iron pipe spilling water out of the hillside into a stream. However, the water from it is delicious and local people come here to get supplies.

> The pond, covered in water lilies and surrounded by reeds, is called **la Gouille au Morts** ('water of the dead'), so named because a man got caught up in the ropes of the millstone he was hauling, fell into the water and drowned.

Continue straight on towards Meulières à Vachat, through bushes, to reach the next signpost 'la Pierre au Mort' (30min). Turn right to Meulières à Vachat/Places des Danses/Crêtes de Vouan on a sunken track winding upwards through woodland. After 15mins there is a large sign saying 'Meulières de Vouan' indicating Meulières à **Vachat** 5min to the right. This narrow path takes you to a big quarry where you can see imprints of the millstones (*meules*) which were cut out of the solid rock, leaving a series of cave-like structures (55min).

Go back to the signpost and continue up towards Places des Danses on a winding track which steepens to reach a clearing called Places des Danses at a T-junction. Turn right towards Crête de Chauffemérande/Crêtes de Vouan to reach another signpost. Go up left on a narrow path which goes up and along a tree-covered ridge to signposts at Cri de Chardieu (925m). Continue straight on the path, which becomes wider and flatter going through tall pines, until you reach the signpost 'Crête de Chauffemérande – alt. 920m' (1hr 30min).

There are lots of bilberry bushes along here, so it is a good place to come in autumn as the berries make delicious tarts. In summer look out for the small chanterelle mushrooms.

Take the narrow path up right towards Crêtes de Vouan/Trin Trin/Sardagne/Sevraz and walk along the crest of the ridge where you can see cliffs to the right. ◄ Still undulating along this attractive wooded ridge you come to a sort of crossroads in a clearing with a sign saying 'les Cinq Chemins' ('the five-ways') ❶ (1hr 50min).

Continue straight, even though the signpost to Crêtes de Vouan looks as if it is indicating right. This is a steep path with lots of tree roots going up to the top of a hump and then undulating along the Vouan ridge.

> From the **Crêtes de Vouan** there are lovely views, especially if the leaves are off the trees. To the left you can catch a glimpse of the snowy Mont Blanc massif and the Dents du Midi, while nearer is the solitary peak of the Môle. To the right are extensive views of the Lake Geneva basin and the southern side of the Salève, with the Jura behind. You can also see the village of Mijouet in the valley below, with the buildings of a holiday centre on the hill behind.

After about 15mins you reach a large flat rock on the edge of the ridge, which is an excellent place for a picnic. After this the path descends very abruptly so you have to be careful where you put your feet. Look out for the yellow arrows on green on this section. It then levels out again to reach a wider path and a T-junction at a sign-post headed 'Crêtes de Vouan' ❷ (2hr 10min). Here you part company with the signposts for a while, and the path is not so easy to find.

Go right where there are no indications (left says 'Trin Trin/Sardagne', but do not take it). This is a nar-row, rather overgrown track that goes steeply down to the left. There is a short, slightly tricky section here as the path goes down a steep eroded gully, so go down carefully, especially if it has just rained or is very dry. Here the path looks as though it continues to the right, but in fact it does go down the gully. After 5mins, look out for an old wooden signpost pointing back up to the Crêtes de Vouan, at a sharp right-hand bend going down steeply. This is not easy to see, so make sure you do not miss it.

Millstone imprints at la Grande Gueule

There is a **detour** out onto a rocky promontory just after the left side of the bend. It gives a magnificent view down the Vallée de l'Arve as far as Geneva, but do not go too near the edge as there is a sharp drop.

Turn sharp right at the bend and continue down – the trees have been felled on this slope so there are good views. Continue down and round a hairpin bend into denser woodland to reach a signpost indicating left to Meulières de la Grande Gueule ❸ (2hr 40min). The path descends fairly steeply, with a protective fence for part of the way, to reach another ancient quarry with millstones cut out of the rock, many of them now disfigured with grafitti. ◀

This is a more impressive cave-like grotto, which resembles its name ('big mouth').

Retrace your steps to the signpost at ❸ and bear down left to reach a junction with a signpost headed 'Sous Grande Gueule'. Turn left towards Boisinges and continue through woodland until you reach two signposts at Vouan (685m). Turn right and descend to the parking at la Source qui Rit (3hr 15min).

WALK 9

Pointe de Miribel

Start/Finish	Villard, 795m
Distance	13km
Total ascent	790m
Grade	Medium
Time	4hr 45min
Maximum altitude	1580m
Map	IGN 3429 ET Bonneville/Cluses1:25,000
Access	From Boëge, turn right in front of the church and then left onto the D22 to Villard. Park your car in the car park at the entrance to Villard on the left, in front of the Mairie (town hall) and school.
Signposting	Good after Plaine Joux, with new signposts and posts with yellow arrows on green, but you need to follow the route directions carefully before that as there are only a few old wooden signposts, which are difficult to read, and some faded red and blue paint splashes

This is a very pleasant walk, with extended views over rolling, tree-covered hills and countryside typical of the Vallée Verte, past attractive farms and scattered hamlets bright with flowers in the summer months. Although fairly long it is not too demanding, except for the short, rocky scramble down from the Pointe itself. This is a popular area for both cross-country skiing in winter and for walking in summer, and you may meet lots of people climbing up to the Pointe, most of whom start from the nearby car park. The panorama from the summit is spectacular, with views of the peaks above Lake Geneva to those above Lac d'Annecy, with Mont Blanc towering behind.

The **Pointe de Mirabel** is one of the many peaks in the area with a statue of the Virgin Mary on the summit, erected in 1878 to replace the large wooden cross put up in 1774. Leading to it are 17 Stations of the Cross in different styles, hewn out

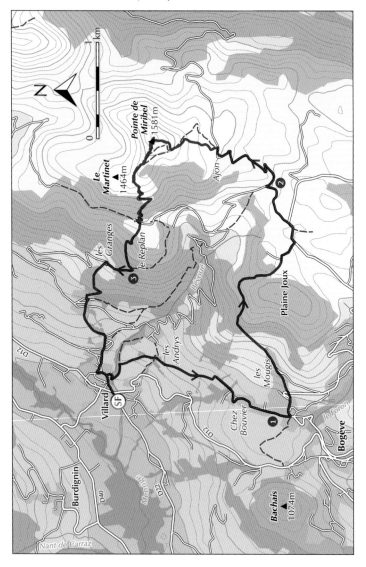

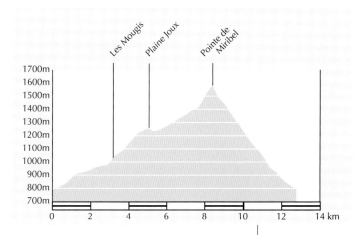

of red marble in 1804 by a local sculptor named
Joseph Marie Felisaz. All he required in payment
was his food to be brought to him each day.

From the signpost at the car park (796m), turn left up the
road towards le Replon/la Glappaz/Pointe de Mirabel/
Ajon. Cross the road and almost immediately turn right
into the Route de la Veillaz Devant following the road
sign to le Bourgeau/les Noyers. After about 100 metres,
opposite an old stone trough on the left, take the smaller
road to the right, the Route de Badosse. After another
100 metres, take the next road on the right which goes
between an iron crucifix on the left and house number
166, named la Badosse, on the right. Shortly after, at an
old farm, the road bears to the right and becomes a track
which crosses a stream to enter trees. This narrow track
bears left at a red arrow and winds up round a field and
orchard, bearing to the right. ▶ You reach the first house
of **les Andrys** on the left, where there is a metal cross
on a concrete base with the inscription 'Souvenir de la
Mission Decembre 1936' (20min).
   Opposite the cross there is an old wooden signpost
(almost hidden in the trees) saying 'les Andrys', at the

Here there are lovely
views across the
wooded hills and
scattered hamlets
of the Vallée Verte.

103

start of a narrow path going to the right into the trees. Turn onto this path, which gains height very gradually until you come to a farm, where it becomes paved. Turn right and continue on the paved road to another farm and bear left to reach an old wooden signpost headed 'Chez Bovet – alt. 962m', which points back to les Andrys and Villard. Continue up the road between houses to reach a small stone fountain on the left, dated 1880. The road bears to the right into **Chez Bouvier**. Continue along the road, passing a small shrine on the left, to reach a bigger road, the D190B, at the hamlet of les Lavouets where there is a cross and a new signpost ❶ (50min).

Turn left, following the signs to les Mougis/la Fargueusaz/Plaine Joux. Continue up the road past some attractive old houses and, where it bends to the left, take a short cut to the left of a small stone shrine to St Joseph, built 1848, with a new plaque dated 2001. A couple of minutes later you cross the same road and cut up again on a fairly steep path through the woods to reach a paved road at a farm. Continue up the road to a T-junction at a crucifix on a stone plinth, with 'Souvenir du Jubilee 1901' written on it, and walk up through the scattered houses of **les Mougis** to the end of the hamlet (1hr 15min).

Where the road bends to the right at a hairpin bend, just before an iron crucifix, take the grassy track to the left, which winds up through fields with extended views over the Vallée Verte to the left. The path becomes stony and enters coniferous and beech woods to meet another path joining from the right. Continue upwards between high banks to reach an open clearing surrounded by fir trees. Walk across the clearing to a wooden signpost at the far side and follow the sign straight on towards Plaine Joux into open meadows. Continue past some chalets to a small road where you turn down right to join a larger road at a T-junction by the Restaurant l'Alpage (1hr 55min).

Turn left along the road, past a wooden signpost at **Plaine Joux** (1263m), and follow the signs to Ajon/Miribel. ◀ The road is the Route du Plaine Joux, and is signposted to Villard. It winds up past more buildings and a big car park on the right, which serves the cross-country

You can see the Pointe de Miribel with the statue on it straight ahead.

Looking up to the Pointe from Ajon

ski area of Plaine Joux, to arrive at two farms and shortly after at a junction, where there is a new signpost 'le Borbieu – alt. 1338m' ❷ (2hr 10min). ▶

Following the signs to Ajon/Pointe de Miribel, walk up the road to the car park at **Ajon**, cutting off the final corner to reach the picnic tables and signpost (2hr 35min). Turn left and take the track to the summit, which climbs steeply up grassy slopes for about 20mins before reaching the first of the Stations of the Cross, where there is an information board. Continue up past the 17 Stations of the Cross, which end in a short scramble up a rocky gulley to come out at a signpost just below the statue of the Virgin at the summit of the **Pointe de Miribel** (3hr 10min).

From here there is an easy walk back to Villard if you decide not to go up the Pointe de Miribel.

From the **Pointe de Miribel** there is a glorious panorama of the surrounding mountains. On your left to the east are the high peaks of the Chablais above Lake Geneva, including the Cornettes de Bise, Dents du Midi and Roc d'Enfer; on the right to the west are the Tournette and Parmelan above Lac d'Annecy; and in the centre the Mont Blanc massif dominates all. It is worth going down to the orientation table just below the summit, where the names of all the surrounding peaks are listed. This is the ideal place for a picnic.

From the signpost just before the statue, follow signs to le Replan/les Granges/les Crozats/Villard. Walk in front of the statue to the other side of the summit and look for faint blue paint splashes indicating a narrow path going downwards over the rocks. This is a short, steep scramble of about 5mins, and you can see the path below you. When you get to where the path flattens, there is a signpost 'Sous-Mirabel – alt. 1550m', which points back to another path to Ajon going back hard left. Continue straight on along the ridge to reach a post with a yellow arrow at a junction. Bear right and go through two fences down the slope. In early summer there are several species of orchids along this path, including early purple, common spotted, burnt and military. The path then contours round to the left to reach a low pass and signpost 'le Martinet – alt. 1450m'. Do not go up the hump of **le Martinet** just to the right, but continue straight on past a large stone with a blue circle on it and then an old stone water trough beside a modern iron basin. ◄

On the right across the valley is the Montagne d'Hirmentaz and on the left the tree-covered Tête des Cudres.

Follow the path downhill to reach a post with a green top and bear left to wind down through scattered woodland. At a fork with an old wooden signpost pointing back up to Ajon/Miribel and a post with a yellow arrow

Stations of the Cross leading to the statue

on green, bear left on narrow path going steeply down to reach a new signpost at **le Replan** (1294m) (3hr 50min).

The track reaches a road at a house and a barn where it bends right and then left to another signpost where you take a narrow path in trees going down towards les Granges. The path crosses a field beside a stream, bright with golden marsh marigolds in spring, and then goes back into the woods to reach a T-junction with another track coming in from the left ❺. Turn right here to reach a road at the signpost leading to the farm of **les Granges** (4hr 10min).

Just after the farm buildings, at a signpost headed 'les Granges – alt. 1084m', turn off the road onto a small track to the left going to les Crozats/Villard. The narrow track winds steeply downhill, initially beside a stream and a meadow, into woods full of wild garlic. After reaching a farm, the track meets the road at a signpost 'les Crozats – alt. 945m' (4hr 25min).

Turn left towards Villard and at the next signpost turn right onto the Chemin des Chaffeux, passing a stone cross. Continue downhill through the houses to the road. Cross over and go down the track leading to a house on the left and another signpost 'les Crozats – alt. 930m'. Turn left towards Villard par le Bourgeau on an unsurfaced road. Shortly after, at a fork, bear right and walk down through the meadows towards the houses of le Bourgeau ahead. You arrive at a signpost 'le Bourgeau – alt. 867m', and an old public wash-house, dated 1902, next to a shirine with a statue of the Virgin, dated 1799, and two curious oriental heads below it. Continue straight down from here across the road, past a concrete pylon with a blue splash on it, to an intersection, and continue straight on past the farm on the right and a cross on the left. Make for the church of Villard, which is visible ahead. Take the turning left in front of the church, at a post with a yellow arrow, and make your way back through **Villard** down to the town hall where your car is parked (4hr 45min).

WALK 10
Montagne d'Hirmentaz

Start/Finish	Télésiège la Frastaz, Habère-Poche, 1085m
Distance	9.5km
Total ascent	550m
Grade	Medium
Time	4hr
Maximum altitude	1595m
Map	IGN 3429 ET Bonneville/Cluses 1:25,000
Access	From Boëge, turn right on the D22/D12 towards Villard/Habère-Poche. At the entrance to Habère-Poche take the D22 right towards the Col de Terramont, and after the first hairpin bend take the small road on the right to park at the Frastaz chairlift.
Signposting	Good in parts – some new signposts and red/yellow markings when on the GRP Tour de la Vallée Verte

The views from the long Hirmentaz ridge are spectacular as it overlooks Lake Geneva and the Jura mountains on one side, and the peaks of the Chablais and Mont Blanc on the other. Although there are some ski installations crisscrossing the slopes as you get higher, they do not detract from the views. The best time to do the walk is in spring and early summer, when you will see an abundance of flowers, especially different species of orchids.

Facing the Frastaz chairlift, turn left along the tarmac road, passing a house on the left and the start of les Crêtes chairlift on the right, to reach the main D22 road at a junction. Turn right up the road to reach the **Col de Terramont** (1100m) (15min).

Continue for a short distance up the road, and opposite the last house on the left look for a signpost on the right indicating Chalets Favier/Crêtes d'Hirmentaz/la Glappaz. Take this undefined path up through a grassy field, and bear right to enter woods. Follow the orange

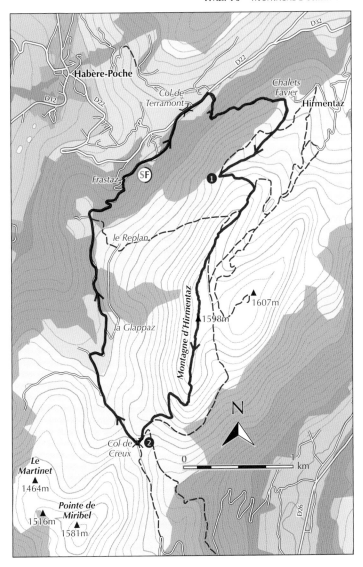

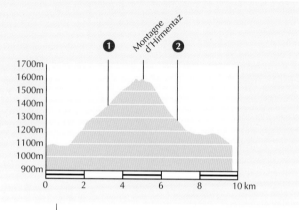

circles up and at a fork bear left. You are climbing fairly steeply on a narrow path which becomes steeper after the signpost headed 'Alt. 1200m'. The path comes out into the open at the **Chalets Favier** on your left and a signpost at 1290m (50min).

Turn right towards Crêtes d'Hirmentaz, keeping the fence on your left. From now on there are no more signposts until you are down at the Col de Creux, so look carefully for red/yellow markings on the rocks – these are not always easy to see. This is a narrow path through grass, which becomes more defined as it bears right towards a shallow valley between low hills. Walk up the middle of this valley to reach an old wooden signpost with a red/yellow marking, indicating le Replan straight on. Turn up to the left to join a grassy track just above a sort of col **①** (1hr 20min). ◀

The track goes up the slope to the left, towards the ski lifts you see ahead. When you are almost at the ridge, bear right alongside a fence to reach the arrival hut for the chairlift of les Crêtes coming up from near where you parked your car. You can now see along the impressive **Montagne d'Hirmentaz** and the path going all the way along the top, with a small lake and a number of ski lifts down in a dip on the left (1hr 45min). Go

From here there is a lovely view down the other side into the Vallée Verte, and in springtime the slopes are dotted with early purple orchids.

Ski tows below the Montagne d'Hirmentaz

up the mound beyond the hut to reach the path going along the ridge.

As you walk along the **Montagne d'Hirmentaz**, you get dramatic views on all sides. Straight ahead and to the left are Mont Blanc and the peaks of the Chablais, and on the right you look across the Vallée Verte to Lake Geneva with the Jura range in the background.

The path is quite narrow but well trodden and clearly signed with red/yellow markings. It undulates along the top with flowers each side, and in some places a steep drop to the right. Just before the highest point there is a track down to the left, which you ignore. Continue along to reach the highest point at a concrete trig marker (1598m) (2hr 10min). This is a good place to stop and have your picnic.

A few minutes later the path begins to drop down to the right of the ridge and then, losing height, crosses a fence and zigzags more steeply down a rather undefined

Walking along the Hirmentaz ridge

On this side of the hill the early purple orchids are magnificent in spring, with carpets of paler common spotted and fragrant orchids later in the year.

path towards a small pond, where cows are grazing in the summer. Directly ahead is the Pointe de Miribel, with a statue of the Virgin Mary on the summit. ◄ At the bottom of the slope the path reaches a chalet at a jeep track. Turn left and walk down the jeep track, passing other chalets, to reach a signpost at the **Col de Creux** ❷ (2hr 50min).

Turn right at the signpost following the sign to Habère-Poche (the jeep track continues left to Ajon/Mégevette/la Combe) on a grassy path through a sort of crease in the hill. This track becomes wide and stony and takes you slightly down and round the mountain to reach a signpost at **la Glappaz** (1205m), at a small parking area and the road coming from le Replan (3hr 5min).

Following the sign to le Replan/Torchebrise/Villard/Chalets Favier, walk down the road, past the Auberge de Miribel on the left (now closed down) and some lovely old farms. At a T-junction and another signpost (la Glappaz – alt. 1176m), turn right towards le Replan/Chalets Favier/Crêtes d'Hirmentaz. Walk down this narrow tarmac road, attractively dotted with chalets and renovated farms. For a while the road goes through woods with a steep drop to the left as you wind back round the bottom of the Hirmentaz to reach the **Frastaz** chairlift and the car park (4hr).

WALK 11
Mont Forchat

Start/Finish	Habère-Poche, 965m
Distance	13.5km
Total ascent	800m
Grade	Medium
Time	5hr 20min
Maximum altitude	1540m
Map	IGN 3428 ET Thonon/Evian 1:25,000
Access	From Boëge, take the D22/D12 towards Col de Cou which goes through Villard and Habère-Lullin to Habère-Poche. In the village of Habère-Poche park your car opposite the Restaurant les Tiennolet.
Signposting	Good – new signposts and wooden posts with yellow arrows on green, some faded yellow splashes and red/white GR markings for the Balcon du Léman

This is an attractive walk with lovely views of the Vallée Verte, the surrounding Chablais peaks and the Mont Blanc massif on the horizon. Although there is a considerable height gain, nothing is very steep, except for the final 100m to the summit of Mont Forchat. The statues on the high points, and the shrine and crucifixes passed on the walk, are testimony of the strong Catholic faith in this area in the 18th and 19th centuries. Although the start is at the small ski resort of Habère-Poche, the walk is on quiet paths and does not go near any of the ski installations.

From the new signpost at the parking area, follow signs to Mont Forchat par Granges Mamet and cross the road to take the narrow Chemin des Molliets upwards. Go up this road, ignoring all side turnings, to reach the signpost at **le Vernay** on a corner (15min).

Continue towards Mont Forchat, and at the next signpost, just before a corner between two houses, take a small tarmac road down to the left, towards le Doucy.

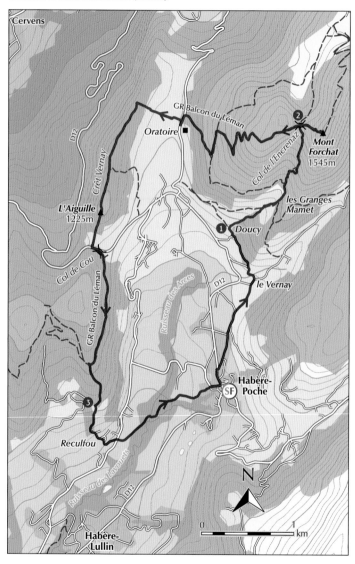

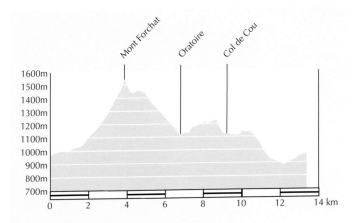

Just before two new houses look for a yellow arrow on the right and turn up this narrow track to reach the road at Doucy Bardet. Turn right on this road towards Mont Forchat, to reach the signpost at **Doucy** (1042m) ❶.

At the signpost, go up the main jeep track, following the signs to Col de l'Encrenaz/Mont Forchat. This is

View from Mont Forchat

115

From the Col de l'Encrenaz you look down to a group of chalets called Très le Mont in a grassy valley, with Lake Geneva and the town of Thonon beyond.

a *route forestière*, used by logging vehicles, and may be muddy after a lot of rain. Stay on the track until you reach a signpost 'les Esserts – alt. 1089m', where you turn sharp right. The track passes **les Granges Mamet** (1159m) on the left, and at the signpost headed 'Alt. 1200m' you ignore a track off to the right which goes to Granges Michaux. Climb steeply through the forest until you come out into the open at a signpost at **Col de l'Encrenaz** ❷ where you will return after climbing Mont Forchat (1hr 45min). ◄

Turn right at the signpost and make your way up the steep, stony path to the summit of **Mont Forchat** (1545m) (2hr).

On the **summit** there is a large white statue of St François de Sales, the saint born at Thorens-Glières in 1567, who was given the task of re-converting the Haute Savoie back to Catholicism after the

Statue of St François de Sales

Reformation. The statue was erected by the parish of Lullin in 1898, when it was fashionable to build statues on the summits of mountains.

From here there is a magnificent view to the south of the rolling hills of the Vallée Verte, the surrounding peaks of the Chablais area, including the Dents du Midi, and the Mont Blanc massif in the background, and to the north Lake Geneva with the Jura mountains on the horizon. This is a perfect picnic spot.

Walk back down to the Col de l'Encrenaz ❷ and take the path straight on towards Col des Moises/Col de Cou. You are now on the **GR Balcon du Léman** indicated by red/white markings. This is a pleasant path through fir trees, which zig-zags gently down as it contours round the mountain to reach a signpost headed 'Alt. 1321'. Turn right towards Col des Moises/Col de Cou to reach a junction at Creux de la Marlat (1211m). Bear down right through the woods until you arrive at a tarmac road by a signpost 'Col des Moises – alt. 1115m' (3hr). Take a moment to visit a small *oratoire* about 20 metres down the road on the left-hand side.

The **Oratoire des Moises** is a little square shrine with a cross on the roof. Behind the grille is a statue of Our Lady. The number 1160 is marked on the stone above the statue, but this is an old altitude marker, not the date of the shrine!

Walk back from the shrine to the signpost and follow signs across the road to Col de Cou (you are still on the Balcon du Léman). The grassy path crosses a marshy area beside the end of a glider take-off area and there is a notice warning of danger if gliders are taking off (*Vol de Planeurs*). Go towards the woods where there is a wooden signpost, pointing left to Habère-Poche and right to les Moises. Do not take these, but go straight across into the woods to pass a red/white GR sign. The path climbs steeply up through the woods following the red/

white markings and yellow splashes, bearing left at a GR sign when you are almost at the top (3hr 15min).

You are now walking along the wooded ridge of the **Crêt Vernay** on an easy path, although for part of the way there is a sharp drop to your right. Continue until you finally come out into the open at the end of the ridge at **L'Aiguille** (1225m), by a signpost and a gold-painted statue of the Virgin Mary.

> The **statue of the Virgin** was erected in 1879 and the inscription on it says that an indulgence of 40 days is granted to those who recite three hail Marys at this spot. From here there is a good view to the north over the lake with the Jura range on the horizon – you can also see Geneva and the Jet d'Eau. On the left is the long Voirons ridge.

In spring there are common spotted orchids at the side of this path.

Before you is a long grassy path which goes down a slope and meets the road at the **Col de Cou** (4hr). ◄ At the Col de Cou there are a few chalets and a restaurant to the right. Following the sign to Reculfou, turn left on the road downwards and then take the first path on the right signposted to Reculfou, still following the red/white GR signs. Continue on the wide track curling round the side of a wooded slope with lovely views all around, including of Mont Forchat to the left. You come to a four-way junction at the signpost 'les Cricolets – alt. 1100m'.

This is where you leave the Balcon du Léman and the GR signs. Go down to the left following the yellow splashes and signs towards les Grands Clos/Reculfou. Keep to the main path, which at first is rocky and stony, going steeply down through woods, until you see a large building on a tarmac road. This is les Grands Clos and from here you can see the hamlet of Reculfou down on the left ❺ (4hr 35min).

Just before the building look for a narrow track to the left (no sign) and follow this to go down below the building beside a fence, initially with a field on your left. The path is fairly steep, and then goes into a beech wood with a stream on the right (a few yellow splashes), to reach the tarmac road and the hamlet of **Reculfou** (920m) at an old wooden signpost. Follow the road into the village, towards Habère-Poche (4hr 45min).

At a fork by a cross go right, round a beautiful old farm in the bend, and continue down to another wooden signpost to reach the main road by a smaller cross on the left, erected in 1875. Cross the road and go straight ahead (no sign). You are now on the valley floor and walking on a tarmac road through fields – you can see the Hirmentaz ridge straight ahead with Mont Forchat to the far left and the Pointe de Miribel on the right. Continue to a sewage plant on the right.

Go straight past the sewage plant (do not follow the path round to the right) and cross the **Lavouets/Arces** stream just beyond a house called Moulin Neuf, with an old millstone in the garden. Just after the house, there is a signpost where you go straight ahead towards Habère-Poche, up into beech woods. This is the last uphill of the day and, although only short, can seem endless when the sun is beating down. Eventually you see the church with its tall steeple ahead. Make for the church, going gently uphill towards **Habère-Poche**. You pass the cemetery and church on the left and then the town hall on the right before meeting a narrow road where you turn up right to meet the main road through the village. Turn left towards the Restaurant les Tiennolet and a welcome drink (5hr 20min).

Overlooking Habère Poche

VALLEE DU BREVON

The pastures of les Charmettes (Walk 16)

The Vallée du Brevon lies to the east of the Vallée Verte, the Brevon being the lesser of the three tributaries of the Dranse, the main ones coming from the Val d'Abondance and Val de Morzine. The three meet at Bioge from where the river crashes through a winding gorge, popular for white-water rafting and canyoning, into a delta near Thonon-les-Bains. The Brevon used to be the haunt of beavers, and the name comes from *bièvre*, an Old French word for beaver. The Vallée du Brevon is less well known than the other two valleys of the Dranse, and remains relatively unspoilt. As with the rest of the Chablais, this is a very Catholic area

where you will find shrines and small chapels, even in the most remote spots, where masses are still held in summer to bless the flocks.

Coming into the valley from either the Vallée Verte or Thonon-les-Bains in the north, you first reach Mont d'Hermone, where there is a lovely ridge walk on part of the long-distance footpath of the Balcon du Léman, giving spectacular views of Lake Geneva. Continuing south, you soon reach the small resort Bellevaux, the main town in the valley, which is linked with the ski slopes of Hirmentaz. To the east of Bellevaux are two very different, although equally lovely walks: one up the grassy, wooded Pointe de la Gay and the other up the rocky cliffs of the Nifflon. The Nifflon is a limestone area where rainwater filters underground, resulting in very rich pastures for the cows and sheep which graze here.

Further up the valley is the attractive Lac de Vallon, created in 1943 when an enormous landslide below the Pointe de la Gay formed a natural dam across the Brevon and destroyed 15 chalets and three sawmills, completely drowning the hamlet of l'Econduit. The lake is now a popular picnic spot for families, and on its shores is the tiny chapel of St Bruno, all that remains of the Chartreuse de Vallon, a Carthusian monastery built in 1136 and destroyed at the time of the Reformation. At the end of the lake is the hamlet of la Chèvrerie, a secluded spot where several walks start. One is up to the Pointe de Chalune, beneath the massive bulk of the Roc d'Enfer, a mountain that is not easy to climb. The Brevon river has its source here, welling out of the rocks in a quiet spot in the woods on the way up to the Pointe.

The nearby summits of the Haute Pointe and Pointe d'Uble are also beneath the Roc d'Enfer, but are more easily accessible from the Giffre river valley in the south. This is a quiet pastoral area, with cows grazing in fields around small farms, and meadows studded with flowers in spring and summer. The views from all these summits are spectacular, and you will rarely have to share them with other walkers.

The driving directions for walks in this section are from Bellevaux or St-Jeoire.

Roc d'Enfer from the Pointe de Chalune (Walk 15): photo Sharon Bryand

WALK 12

Mont d'Hermone

Start/Finish	Reyvroz, 830m
Distance	10.5km
Total ascent	685m
Grade	Medium
Time	4hr
Maximum altitude	1420m
Map	IGN 3428 ET Thonon/Evian 1:25,000
Access	From Bellevaux, take the D26 through Vailly to Reyvroz, and once there drive up the hill and park your car in front of the church where there is a big white statue of the Virgin Mary.
Signposting	Good – new signposts at the start and older wooden signposts later, red/white GR markings for the Balcon du Léman, and yellow splashes

After a short climb up through trees, this is a delightful ridge walk in a relatively unspoilt area, with extensive views of the surrounding Chablais countryside and peaks, as well as of Lake Geneva with the Jura mountains on the skyline. This is a very Catholic area, and the walk leads to the Stations of the Cross at the small chapel of Notre Dame d'Hermone, where open-air masses are still held. This was the author's favourite walk in the Haute Savoie, and the last she did before she died.

Before you set off, look at the information board next to the church, which has a map of the peaks of the Chablais.

◄ As you face the church go straight up the road keeping the church on your right (do not go left to le Bulle, Lanversin). There are red/white GR signs on electricity poles nearby as this is part of the Balcon du Léman. The road goes briefly between old stone walls, and comes to a little shrine called l'Oratoire des Pas, dated 1723. Inside there is a statue of the Virgin Mary.

At the signpost headed 'l'Oratoire – alt. 800m' just before the shrine, go up left towards Montagne des Soeurs/ Mt d'Hermone/Chapelle d'Hermone. This is a wide jeep track going up steeply for 400m through bushes and light

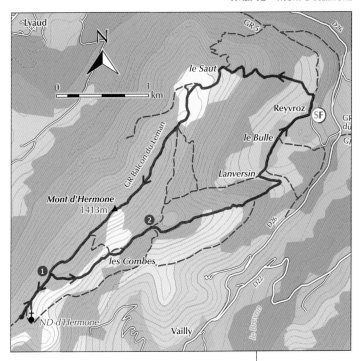

woodland. Down on the left there is a lovely view of
Reyvroz and the church. Keep straight on this jeep track
following red/white markings and yellow arrows on green
(ignore the path off to the right marked 'Voie sans Issue').
You enter a zone of coniferous trees, and later there is a
fork right with a red/white warning cross to the left. The
track winds upwards. Continue straight up at a small crossroads (there is a power line here), going through a fence
and reaching a clearing with a big barn on the left and a
signpost at **le Saut** (1150m) (55min).

Following the signs to Montagne des Soeurs/Mont
d'Hermone, cross the clearing on the main track. Shortly
afterwards you come onto the open pastureland of Mont
d'Hermone.

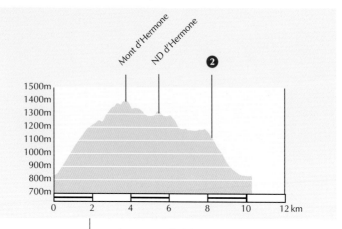

This is now called the **Montagne des Soeurs** (mountain of the nuns) but in the 11th century it was called the Chemin des Chartreux, as the Carthusian monks used to cross here when they were going from their monastery near Lac Vallon to their property in Thonon.

Continue straight on the track – there is a cross on the top of the hill to your right – to reach a signpost 'Montagne des Soeurs – alt. 1217m' next to a chalet, with a TV transmitter and a small hut beyond. Following the sign to Chapelle d'Hermone, turn left in front of the chalet on a wide grassy track (red/white markings), which goes up the hill, shortly joining a potentially muddy jeep track. This takes you through a fence into coniferous wood and an intersection at another signpost 'Montagne des Soeurs – alt. 1250m' (1hr 10min).

Go left towards Mt d'Hermone/Chapelle d'Hermone following the red/white markings. Some 100 metres further on there is a signpost headed 'Alt. 1260m' indicating straight on to Mont d'Hermone (left goes to Vailly/Reyvroz). A few metres later at a fork go left, still on the jeep track. You are now climbing up in a series of steep switchbacks along a very wide ridge through woodland

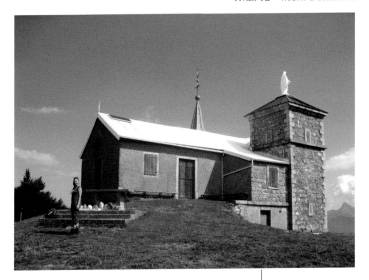

Chapel of Notre Dame d'Hermone

and bushes. Keep to the main upward path until you come out in the open to reach the highest point of the ridge of **Mont d'Hermone** (1413m) where there is a wooden sign (1hr 40min).

> From **Mont d'Hermone** there are extended views to the right and left. To the right you look over Lake Geneva with the Jura mountains on the horizon, and to the left, beyond the valley, are the peaks of the Chablais: the Dent d'Oche, Cornettes de Bise, Mont Chauffé, Mont Billiat, Pointe d'Ireuse and Rocher de Nifflon. In the foreground, over to the right, is the Montagne d'Hirmentaz in the Vallée Verte.

The path undulates along the top of the ridge, dropping down through tall pine forest and then up again, to reach a wooden signpost headed 'les Combes – alt. 1350m' ❶ (1hr 55min). Left goes to the chalets of les Combes, which is 10mins further, and is the path you will take on your return. Keep straight on towards Chapelle d'Hermone,

Lunch stop at the chapel

Alternatively you can continue for a few minutes into woodland until you come to a path going sharply up left by the Stations of the Cross, which were put up in 1842. Follow them (the path joins at the tenth station) up to the chapel.

passing a wooden signpost indicating left to le Plansuet/ Vailly. Shortly after a windsock for paragliding, the **Chapel of Notre Dame d'Hermone** is visible on your left and you can go to it directly up a grassy path (2hr 15min). ◄

CHAPEL OF NOTRE DAME D'HERMONE

The Chapel of Notre Dame d'Hermone is situated on an open spur at the end of the Mont d'Hermone ridge and has a beautiful uninterrupted view. It has a steeple with a cross, and on top an impressive weather vane in the shape of a cockerel – rather a pagan finish, but typical of many churches in this region. On the roof is an imposing white statue of Our Lady and at the side a more modern cross with '1975 Année de la Reconciliation' marked on it. There is also an outside stone altar, and it is still the custom on Whitsunday, on the Feast of the Assumption (15 August) and on Our Lady's Birthday (8 September) for people to follow the Stations of the Cross up to the church and then hear open-air mass.

For 500 years a chapel has stood on this spot, although it has been destroyed and rebuilt several times over the centuries. More recently it was renovated in 1979 and the old doors were replaced in 1989, the year of its centenary. Take time to read the two poems attached to the door. The first, entitled 'Aujourd'hui est à Toi', reminds you of the importance of making the most of today; the second, entitled 'Prendre le Temps', reminds you of the importance of taking time to reflect, to listen, to relax, to love and to pray.

From the signpost 'Chapelle d'Hermone – alt. 1326m' (just below the chapel towards the Stations of the Cross) follow the signs to Mont d'Hermone/Reyvroz and retrace your steps back along the ridge to the wooden signpost headed 'les Combes' ❶. Take the second turning down on your right to les Combes/Reyvroz, following the yellow splashes carefully. The path winds back round the contour of the mountain through bushes and then coniferous woods alternating with open spaces, and then goes in front of an abandoned barn before reaching a junction with a wooden signpost indicating left to **les Combes** and straight on to Reyvroz (2hr 45min). ▸

It is worth going up to have at look at les Combes, which consists of a few old farm buildings, and is situated on a lovely open shelf in the hillside.

Go straight on, towards Reyvroz. The path continues round the contour of the hill and there are bare patches of hillside where the trees have been taken for logging (all replanted with fir saplings), followed by dense patches of conifers. You come to a wooden signpost at a sort of crossroads ❷. Following the sign indicating 'Reyvroz par les 2 Sapins', continue straight on, onto a narrow grassy path marked by yellow splashes. It is still winding round the mountain through patches of dense coniferous wood and reaches a wooden signpost (3hr 30min).

Go right towards Reyvroz, on a path going steeply down through beech wood, to reach a fence on your right with open fields beyond and a big barn. Do not bear right

The hunting weather vane at Lanversin

into the field but continue straight, following the ridge steeply down through continuing beech wood; the path is not very obvious so look out for the yellow circles. You emerge onto a wide track leading to the meadow and barn up on the right. Do not take this but go down to the left (clearly signed) and a few minutes later follow the wooden signpost straight on towards Reyvroz (left goes to Chenoz, back up to les Combes/Notre Dame d'Hermone). Continue down this steep path, following the signs to Reyvroz and going straight at a crossroads. You then come to a wooden chalet called les Deux Sapins, aptly named after the two big fir trees on your right.

> From **les Deux Sapins** you have a lovely view of the little village of Reyvroz, dominated by its church down below on the left, with the ridge of Pic des Mémises and Pic Boré behind. There is also a magnificent view of the twin peaks of the Dent d'Oche.

Continue down left on the wide track to a T-junction where you bear right at the bottom by some dilapidated old wooden signposts that are difficult to read. You pass through the lovely old farm buildings of **Lanversin**. ◄ You then come to a tarmac road. Walk through the hamlets of **le Bulle** and Chez le Gaud to arrive at the village of **Reyvroz** (4hr).

Look out for the amusing weather vane depicting a hunter firing at two wild boar, chased by a hunting dog.

WALK 13
Rocher de Nifflon

Start/Finish	L'Ermont, 1010m
Distance	9km
Total ascent	760m
Grade	Medium
Time	4hr 30min
Maximum altitude	1775m
Map	IGN 3428 ET Thonon/Evian 1:25,000
Access	From Bellevaux, turn left in front of the church and immediately after, turn right on a narrow road at small wooden signposts indicating Pâques and le Frêne. Go along this winding road for about 4km, through the hamlets of Pâques and le Frêne. Cross the bridge at the entrance to l'Ermont and continue to the end of the road where there is space for parking on the left.
Signposting	Good – new signposts and yellow splashes

This is a beautiful walk with magnificent views in a really unspoilt area of the Haute Savoie, passing attractive old chalets and a tiny chapel high on the mountain. The Nifflon is very different from the rounded, wooded Pointe de la Gay nearby, for it is a rocky limestone mountain, the name deriving from the Latin *nec fluere*, meaning 'no flowing water'. The rainwater filters underground through large rocky holes, called *tannes*, where snow collects in winter and lingers throughout the year. The lack of water in dry summers was a problem for farmers who brought their animals up here to graze, and they constructed ladders to collect snow from these holes, one of which you pass on the walk.

Cross the road to the four signposts, and turn right towards les Nants/Col de la Balme/Nifflon d'en Haut par le col de la Balme. ▶ Walk through the hamlet of l'Ermont and at the last of the houses the road becomes a jeep track. After 5mins, it joins up with another jeep track

The track to the left indicating Nifflon d'en Bas/Nifflon d'en Haut is the way you will return.

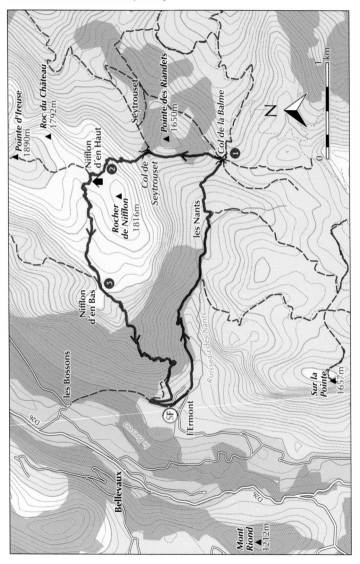

coming up from the right, at a wooden signpost pointing back to l'Ermont. The woods slope upwards on the left and the **Ruisseau des Nants**, often dry, flows through a ravine on the right. Continue along the jeep track to pass a small chalet on a corner and then a pretty little shrine, the Oratoire de la Dent.

> The notice on the **Oratoire de la Dent**, built in the 16th century and restored in 2007, tells you that it was built to atone for the murder of the last Protestant pastor of Bellevue, killed on this spot when the Haute Savoie was converted back to Catholicism after the Reformation.

Soon after you reach a signpost where you go straight ahead towards les Nants/Col de Balme/Nifflon (40min). ▶ Here the stream crosses under the track, and is now on your left as you go through an attractive gorge which then levels out into a narrow valley with meadows and the large rocky mountain of the Rocher de Nifflon on

The track to the right leads to la Ficlaz/ Chalets de Tré le Saix, which is the return route from Walk 14.

Rocher de Nifflon from les Nants

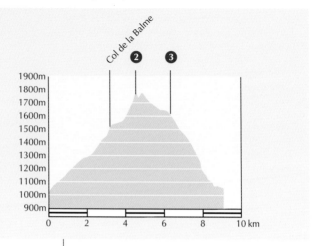

the left. You arrive at the chalets of **les Nants** and, after crossing a metal bridge, there is a signpost headed 'les Nants – alt. 1300m', in front of an old barn just before the road bears to the left (1hr).

Turn left following the sign Col de la Balme/Nifflon d'en Haut/Pointe de la Gay (right goes to Tré le Saix). This is a narrow, fairly steep path, with a row of firs on the right, which reaches a meadow with an attractive old chalet on the left. Follow up the slope of the meadow to a wooden signpost. Do not follow the sign saying 'Nifflon Direct', but go towards Col de Balme/Nifflon par le Col de la Balme, and after about 200 metres you will come to a wooden signpost on a tree pointing up to Col de la Balme. The path climbs up through coniferous forest, steeply in places, to the signpost at **Col de la Balme** (1445m) ❶ (1hr 30min).

The **Col de la Balme** is an open shelf with high grass and lots of flowers in summer, and a small wooden chalet to the left. The walk up the Pointe de la Gay (Walk 14) goes off to the right here. Below is the village of Seytrouset and straight ahead is a magnificent view of the high peaks of the Chablais, including the Cornettes de Bise, Mont Chauffé and Mont de Grange, with the Dents du Midi on the horizon.

At the signpost, turn left past the chalet to reach the next signpost and take the left fork towards Seytrouset par Col de Seytrouset/Nifflon d'en Haut. ▶ This is a narrow path that climbs up fairly steeply through meadows full of flowers, and then enters woods, with lots of knotted tree roots, but is well defined and clearly marked with yellow splashes. It levels out and curls round the mountain, with lovely views through the trees over the Vallée du Brevon. Just after a post with a yellow arrow you come out into an open meadow and the signpost at **Col de Seytrouset** (1564m), with the imposing Rocher de Nifflon to your left (1hr 55min).

Following the signs to Nifflon d'en Haut, turn left on a narrow path going up beside a fence. The path climbs steeply up the hillside, still clearly marked with yellow splashes, getting nearer and nearer to the rocky surface of the Rocher de Nifflon, with the chalets of Seytrouset directly below. As you climb higher, the path gets rockier

Do not take the fork to the right, which also indicates Seytrouset, but not by the col.

Chablais peaks from Rocher de Nifflon

and bends to the right to reach a small col at the top of the steep bit ❷ (2hr 40min).

> The highest point of the **Rocher de Nifflon** (1816m) is over to the left, but it is rather a scramble to get there and is not included in this route description. The col is a good place for a picnic, as there is a magnificent panorama of all the Chablais peaks, including the Dent d'Oche, Cornettes de Bise, Mont Chauffé, Mont de Grange, Roc d'Enfer and Dents du Midi. You can also see les Diablerets and Mont Blanc, with Lake Geneva in front and the Jura range a dark smudge on the horizon. After the rocky scramble up, it comes as a surprise that the other side the mountain falls gently down to a grassy bowl with a collection of chalets and another ridge beyond.

Take the path down into the grassy bowl, past a post with a yellow top, to reach the tiny chapel and the chalets of **Nifflon d'en Haut** (2hr 50min).

> This little **chapel** was originally constructed in wood in 1796 by the parish priest of Bellevaux, who decided to close the village church at the time of the French Revolution and celebrate mass on the mountain. He dedicated the chapel to Notre Dame des Neiges ('Our Lady of the Snows'), probably because of the numerous snow patches which the shepherds collected to water their flocks. In 1821 the wood was replaced by stone, and in 1886 the chapel was again renovated and the attractive onion-shaped steeple was added, topped with an imposing weather vane in the shape of a cockerel.

Take the path through the chalets, one of which is a small refuge, and up to the signpost 'Nifflon d'en Haut – alt. 1760m'.

> The Refuge de Nifflon has bunks for 10, and is equipped with stove and cooking utensils, but

Chapel of Notre Dame des Neiges at Nifflon d'en Haut

no drinking water. It is unsupervised and the key is available at Bellevaux Tourist Office, **www.alpesduleman.com**.

Go left, following signs to Nifflon d'en Bas/l'Ermont (straight on is indicated Pointe d'Ireuse, which is the peak ahead). The wide path descends steadily to reach a wooden structure labelled 'Tanne à Neige', with an arrow pointing to a tanne 50 metres away.

The information board inside the shelter explains that **tanne** is the local dialect for one of the big rocky holes where snow remained all year. In very dry summers the farmers would lower ladders to climb down into the hole to collect the snow in big wooden barrels, which would then be left on the roofs of their chalets to melt for the animals. This was hard work as a full barrel weighed 80kg, and one cow drank 50 litres of water per day. Despite the lack of water, the pastures are very fertile and the butter from here has a special rich flavour.

135

If you follow the arrow up into the woods, you get to the tanne, which still has a rickety wooden platform part of the way down.

Continue along the path, probably an old mule track, which curls down into a narrow valley. It is a pleasant, rocky walk, sprinkled with coniferous and rowan trees, where you will find lots of flowers and butterflies in summer, and moss, bracken and various mushrooms in autumn. The path levels out through woodland, winding round the side of the mountain, rather like the path coming up, with a lovely view in front of Lake Geneva, and reaches the signpost at **Nifflon d'en Bas** ❺ which is a sort of bowl, open at both ends and consisting of a few chalets and a large wooden cross (3hr 25min).

There is a good **viewpoint** just 40m higher on the rocky promontory up to the right, called the Rochers de la Mache, with another cross on it. From here you can see over Lake Geneva and all the peaks of the Chablais and the Vallée Verte, with the village of Bellevaux down in the valley.

Follow the signs down the path to l'Ermont. The path winds down through grassy meadows and eventually into coniferous woods where it is more defined, with a wooded ravine on the left. As you get lower the path becomes steeper and can be slippery after rain or when covered by leaves. At the signpost 'le Reposoir – alt. 1340m', where there is a view into the valley, bear left, following the signs to l'Ermont (4hr).

The path descends steeply for quite a while until you come out of the woods into meadowland, with a view below of the village of l'Ermont, and then enters steep woodland again. It finally comes out into more meadows to reach a wooden signpost. Turn left (not signed) on a grassy path which meets a jeep track at a signpost at **l'Ermont** (1040m). Continue straight on towards les Nants to reach the four signposts at the start of the walk, where your car is parked (4hr 30min).

WALK 14
Pointe de la Gay

Start/Finish	L'Ermont, 1010m
Distance	12km
Total ascent	830m
Grade	Medium
Time	5hr
Maximum altitude	1800m
Map	IGN 3429 ET Bonneville/Cluses 1:25,000. Note: Bellevaux village is off this map, but not Pointe de la Gay
Access	From Bellevaux, turn left in front of the church and immediately after, turn right on a narrow road at small wooden signposts indicating Pâques and le Frêne. Go along this winding road for about 4km, through the hamlets of Pâques and le Frêne. Cross the bridge at the entrance to l'Ermont and continue to the end of the road where there is space for parking on the left.
Signposting	Adequate – some new signposts, posts with yellow arrows on green and yellow splashes

The Pointe de la Gay is in an unspoilt part of the Haute Savoie, where you will meet few other walkers, even in summer. Although next door to the rocky Rocher de Nifflon, it is a complete contrast as it is a grassy, wooded mountain covered with alpenrose and bilberry bushes, with open alpine pastures on the way back. It is a delightful walk at all times of the year, but especially in summer when there are many flowers – however, it might be wise to wear long trousers as some of the paths go through very long grass. From the summit there are dramatic views of the Mont Blanc massif and the surrounding Chablais peaks, including the Roc d'Enfer. You might even see a golden eagle.

Cross the road to the four signposts, and turn right towards les Nants/Col de la Balme/Nifflon d'en Haut par le col de la Balme. Walk through the hamlet of l'Ermont and at the

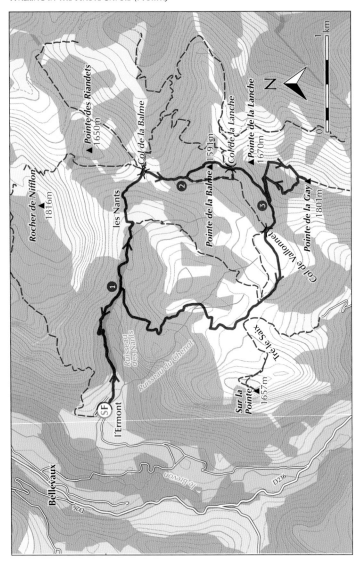

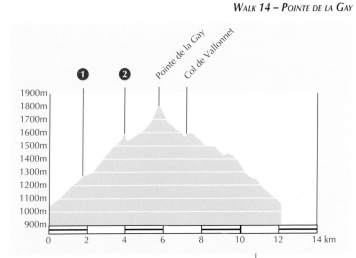

last of the houses the road becomes a jeep track. After 5mins, it joins up with another jeep track coming up from the right, at a wooden signpost pointing back to l'Ermont.

Oratoire de la Dent near l'Ermont: photo Sharon Bryand

The woods slope upwards on the left and the **Ruisseau des Nants**, often dry, flows through a ravine on the right. Continue along the jeep track to pass a small chalet on a corner and then a pretty little shrine.

> The notice on the **Oratoire de la Dent**, built in the 16th century and restored in 2007, tells you that it was built to atone for the murder of the last Protestant pastor of Bellevue, killed at this spot when the Haute Savoie was converted back to Catholicism after the Reformation.

Soon after you reach a signpost ❶ (40min). Continue straight ahead towards les Nants/Col de Balme/Nifflon. ◀ Here the stream crosses under the track, and is now on your left as you go through an attractive gorge which then levels out into a narrow valley with meadows and the large rocky mountain of the Grand Rocher de Nifflon on the left. You arrive at the chalets of **les Nants** and, after crossing a metal bridge, there is a signpost

The track to the right, leading to la Ficlaz/Chalets de Tré le Saix, is the way you will return.

Grassy pastures of Tré la Saix below the Pointe de la Gay: photo Sharon Bryand

headed 'les Nants – alt. 1300m', in front of an old barn just before the road bears to the left (1hr).

Turn left following the sign Col de la Balme/Nifflon d'en Haut/Pointe de la Gay (right goes to Tré le Saix). This is a narrow, fairly steep path, with a row of firs on the right, which reaches a meadow with an attractive old chalet on the left. Follow up the slope of the meadow to a wooden signpost. Ignore the sign saying 'Nifflon Direct', but go towards Col de Balme/Nifflon par le Col de la Balme, and after about 200 metres you will come to wooden signpost on a tree pointing up to Col de la Balme. The path climbs up through coniferous forest, steeply in places, to the **Col de la Balme** (1445m) (1hr 30min).

> The **Col de la Balme** is an open shelf with high grass and lots of flowers in summer, and a small wooden chalet to the left. The walk up the Rocher de Nifflon (Walk 13) goes off to the left here. Below is the village of Seytrouset and straight ahead is a magnificent view of the high peaks of the Chablais, including the Cornettes de Bise, Mont Chauffé and Mont de Grange, with the Dents du Midi on the horizon.

At the signpost turn right, following the sign Col de la Lanche/Col de Vallonnet/Pointe de la Gay. The grassy path climbs upwards between two fences and then through woods, with intermittent red/yellow signs on trees, to reach a signpost headed 'Alt. 1518m', indicating Pointe de la Gay, 1hr 5min. Continue through the woods to a junction of paths ❷ (1hr 40min). There are two possible routes from here to the Col de la Lanche.

Alternative route to the Col de la Lanche
This easier option, taking the right-hand path, goes down through woodland and curls left to reach a clearing with a good view ahead of the Pointe de la Gay. The path is poorly defined across meadowland, but keep slightly left, and then turn left at a signpost up to the **Col de la Lanche** (straight on goes to Col de Vallonnet).

The main route takes the left-hand path which is the more scenic route, although it is steeper and slightly longer. It climbs up to the ridge, with a drop on your left down to the Morzine valley, to reach the rocky **Pointe de la Balme** (1591m), from where you have views up to the Pointe de la Gay. There is then a scramble of about 10m down a steep section with chains for support, certainly needed if the rocks are wet. You arrive at a sort of dip in the mountains, which is the **Col de la Lanche** (1539m) (2hr).

From the Col de la Lanche, continue south, following the wooden sign to Col de Vallonnet/Pointe de la Gay, on a wide new jeep track for about 200 metres before turning off on a small path to your left. This goes upwards and round the **Pointe de la Lanche** through tall coniferous trees with lovely views of the Rocher de Nifflon on the right. It narrows before reaching a signpost 'les Profanfas – alt. 1600m' ❸ (2hr 15min).

Turn left towards Pointe de la Gay. ◄ Follow the path through fir and nut trees to reach open meadowland and a post after a few minutes. Up on the right you have a clear view of your return path down from the summit. Continue straight through open meadowland covered in bilberry bushes until you get to the crest of the hill (the Pointe de la Gay is up on the right and the Pointe de la Lanche on the left) and another lovely view down into the Seytrouset valley. Turn up right, following the line of the hill, and climb about 140m to reach a post with a yellow arrow on green. Continue on for a few metres to reach a signpost at the summit of the **Pointe de la Gay** (2hr 55min).

> Straight on is indicated Col de Vallonnet, and is the way you will go later.

The **summit** is an ideal place for a picnic, with lovely views in all directions. To the north is Lake Geneva with the Jura mountains on the horizon, and to the south the high peaks of the Chablais, with the Mont Blanc massif in the background. Nearby is the rocky ridge of the Rocher de Nifflon with the hamlet of les Nants nestling in the valley below it, and the path continues along the crest past the Col des Follys to the Roc d'Enfer.

Retrace your steps to the post with the yellow arrow and take the narrow path going down to the left. This is a steep path going down the shoulder of the hill, bearing left then right to reach a post in the meadow. It can get rather lost in high summer in the tall flowers and long grass, so follow the occasional yellow splashes carefully. At the post continue down to the signpost at Profanfas ❸ (3hr 15min).

Go left, following the sign Col de Vallonnet/Tré le Saix through a green turnstile. Keep on the path, which becomes a wide track curling down to reach the signpost at **Col de Vallonnet** (1548m), which is a grassy crossroads in a dip (3hr 35min).

Go straight, following the sign to Tré le Saix on a grassy track, which goes up and over a hill. At the top of the hill follow the track left going over the top of a series of bumps in open meadowland until you meet up with a new jeep track. Follow this for about 100 metres until you reach the signpost headed 'Tré le Saix – alt. 1480m'. You can see the chalets of **Tré le Saix** up on your left (4hr).

Follow the signs to l'Ermont crossing the jeep track, and continue over a hump and then down to the forest. You are now on a wide track through scattered woods with a slope to the left down to the **Ruisseau du Chenot**. Continue past a sign indicating left to the Chalet de Ficlaz as the wide rutted track bears round to the right and goes down steeply through beech wood and coniferous trees. Continue to reach the signpost at the original jeep track going up to les Nants ❶ (4hr 30min). Turn left and walk down to where you left the car at **l'Ermont** (5hr).

WALK 15
Pointe de Chalune

Start/Finish	La Chèvrerie, Lac de Vallon, 1120m
Distance	12km
Total ascent	1000m
Grade	Strenuous
Time	6hr
Maximum altitude	2105m
Map	IGN 3429 ET Bonneville/Cluses 1:25,000
Access	From Bellevaux, take the D26 towards St Jeoire and after about 2km take the narrow road going down on the left, indicating Lac de Vallon/la Chèvrerie. Continue past the lake and hamlet of la Chèvrerie, and leave your car in the large parking area of Pont de la Joux where there is a café, the Torchon chairlift and an information board.
Signposting	Mostly good – new signposts and some sporadic yellow and blue markings

This is a long, attractive walk which goes over three passes and gives wonderful views of the whole area between Mont Blanc and Lake Geneva. It goes very close to the dramatic Roc d'Enfer and the source of the River Brevon. The information board at the start of the walk, entitled 'Les Sources du Brevon', has a map of the area, with details of the river and the Lac de Pététoz. It also indicates that you have a good chance of seeing marmots, chamois and moufflons – in fact, there is a large flock of moufflons near the Col de Foron. In spring and early summer look out for gentians, orchids, alpenrose and martagon lilies.

Do not take the wider unpaved track over a green iron bridge – this is where you will come from on your return.

At the Pont de la Joux there are several signposts as it is the starting point for a number of walks. Take the wide track at the side of the chairlift indicating 'Pointe de Chalune par le col de Foron'. ◄ The track gains height gradually, with the River Brevon flowing down on the right. After about 5mins you see the building of **le Finge**

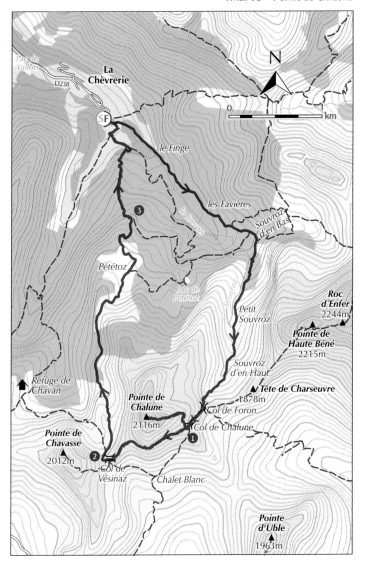

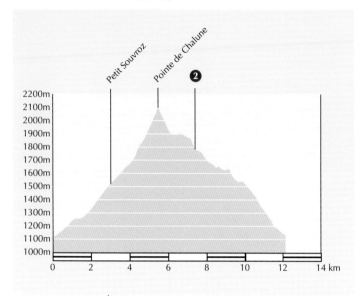

up on the left. Keep straight on, with the stream always on the right, to reach the huts of **les Favières** (25min).

At the crossroads a little further on, go straight over and carry on up the path to the signpost headed 'Alt. 1310m'. Go right towards Source du Brevon/Col de Foron/Roc D'Enfer/Chalune. After crossing the stream the path narrows and becomes stonier to reach the next signpost, which indicates Pointe de Chalune 2hr 40 and Col de Foron 1hr (this is clearly not correct, as the signpost further on indicates that it is 1hr 20min). ◀

The path to the right leads to the nearby source of the Brevon, where the stream wells up from the base of the rocks, and to the Lac de Pététoz.

Continue up the path to the signpost headed 'Alt. 1449m' and go towards the Col de Foron. The path curls round the side of the mountain, beneath the huge cliffs of the **Roc d'Enfer** which tower up on the left. You come out of the woods into an attractive bowl in the mountains, called **Petit Souvroz** (1hr 20min). You have now passed the Roc d'Enfer, which is back on the left, and you can see the Col de Foron up ahead.

This is rocky country, so keep an eye out for **marmots** – they announce their presence by a piercing whistle, which is the marmot sentry's signal to the others that intruders are in the vicinity.

At the signpost 'Petit Souvroz – alt. 1585m', continue straight on towards Pointe de Chalune/Col de Foron. The path crosses the meadows past alder bushes and then begins to zigzag steeply up to the Col de Foron, nearly 250m higher. As you get higher, the slopes on both sides of the path are covered with more and more flowers – alpenrose, gentians, orchids, globe flowers and many more. At the end the path gets much steeper and becomes somewhat eroded and slippery before it reaches the **Col de Foron** (2hr 15min).

From the **Col de Foron** you can see the steep and exposed path along the Roc d'Enfer to your left, with a clear view of the path coming up from the Chalet de Foron, and if you look behind, you can see the way you have walked up from la Chèvrerie.

Roc d'Enfer from the Col de Foron

Ahead are the peaks of the Chablais, with the Dents du Midi and part of the Mont Blanc massif.

Now you can see the summit of Mont Blanc, and to the right you look across to the village of Praz de Lys and the Pointe de Marcelly.

Turn right at the col, following the signpost to Col de Chalune which you can see up on the right as you skirt round the mountain. The path is even more eroded and slippery but it takes only 10mins to reach the **Col de Chalune ❶** (2hr 25min). ◀ Follow the signs to **Pointe de Chalune** on a fairly exposed path which goes steeply up for 220m (3hr 10min).

From the top of the **Pointe de Chalune** there are spectacular views of the surrounding peaks, which include the Pointe d'Uble, Roc d'Enfer, Rocher de Nifflon, Pointe de la Gay and the Môle. The Lac de Roy is down below, with the Pointe de Marcelly ridge behind, and you can see Lake Geneva and the Jura in the distance – there are not many viewpoints where you can see so far in all directions.

Rock formations on the Chalune: photo Sharon Bryand

Looking towards Mont Blanc
from the Col de Chalune

Retrace your steps to the Col de Chalune ❶ and follow the sign to Col de Vésinaz. This is a well-defined path, but towards the end of it, just before the col, you have a big rock to scramble down. ▶ After the big rock you meet the path coming up from Chalet Blanc, and climb up between two rocky peaks, the one on the right a streaky pink colour, to reach the **Col de Vésinaz** ❷ (4hr). From here you get a lovely view of the rocky west side of the Pointe de Chalune.

Go through a green stile to a signpost and follow the signs to Chalets de Pététoz. Walk down the path until you reach the signpost headed 'Alt. 1760m' and go right towards Chalets de Pététoz (to the left is the Col de Chavan, which you cross on Walk 16 up the Haute Pointe). The path goes to the right of a wooded hillock, following blue markings and then yellow ones. You are now walking in a very attractive hanging valley with the rocky cliffs of the Pointe de Chalune to the right. The path goes over a rise and undulates down the valley, which widens as it traverses the hillside, with woods in the valley bottom, and you can see a road across the other

It is also possible to take an easier although longer route between the two cols by continuing down towards Chalet Blanc and then turning right on the path going up to the Col de Vésinaz.

In spring and summer the flowers here are spectacular, especially the gentians.

side. ◄ Continue downhill, past the Col de Jorat, making for the chalets you see below, which are set in beautiful open meadows, to reach **Pététoz** (5hr).

At the signpost at Chalets de Pététoz go towards Pont de La Joux (direct). This goes slightly left in front of the first chalet on a grassy path through meadowland, which takes you by a second chalet called 'Chardons Bleu' (blue thistles). There is an iron cross in the field up right. Enter woodland through another green stile to gain a jeep track through coniferous wood (marked with red/white GR signs), to reach a big open clearing. Take a narrow steep path to the left ❸

This is a short cut; you can stay on the jeep track which is an easier but longer way back.

following a sign indicating la Chèvrerie. ◄ The steep path takes you down to a second clearing. Go straight across and continue downwards. When you see the jeep track ahead, do not try and go through the fence, but keep to the track bending right where there is a way through (signposted back to Pététoz).

Turn left and shortly after you reach an unpaved road and signpost headed 'la Joux – alt. 1141m', where you turn right and follow the signs to Pont de la Joux. Walk across the River Brevon on a green bridge into the parking area in **la Chèvrerie** (6hr).

Trumpet gentians

WALK 16

Haute Pointe

Start/Finish	Sommand, 1410m
Distance	10km
Total ascent	810m
Grade	Medium
Time	4hr 45min
Maximum altitude	1960m
Map	IGN 3429 ET Bonneville/Cluses 1:25,000
Access	From St Jeoire, take the D907 to Mieussy. Go through the village and, at a roundabout just after, take the D308 towards Messy/Sommand/Col de Ramaz. Continue uphill for about 11km to Sommand. Where the main road to Praz de Lys bears left at the Hotel Vacca Park, go straight across towards the large parking area for the ski season and park opposite the hotel.
Signposting	New signposts and posts with yellow arrows on green, as well as some red/yellow and yellow markings

This is a varied walk in unspoilt and peaceful mountain country to the north of Sommand, away from the ski lifts linking with Praz de Lys on the south side. Do not do this walk too early in the season as snow can linger on the steeper north side making walking round impossible. There are three cols to cross and some steep sections, including the rocky scramble up the last few metres to the summit of the Haute Pointe. However, the summit is worth the extra effort as you get a panoramic view of the entire region, including the Mont Blanc massif.

For parts of this walk you are in fenced-off alpine pastures where no dogs are allowed, even on a lead, and where the flocks are guarded by large white dogs called *pastous*. Do not get near these as they are brought up to protect the sheep, and will attack if provoked.

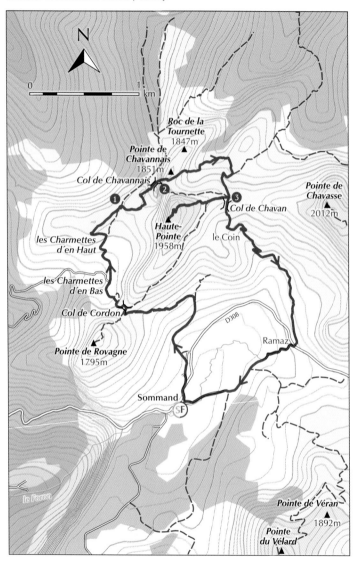

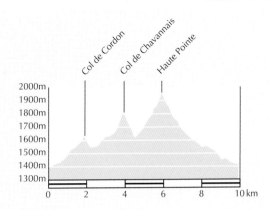

▶ At the Hotel Vacca Park, turn right and walk up the Route du Col de Ramaz for about 100 metres to the restaurant 'le Matafan'. At a yellow arrow on green, leave the main road and take the road on the left. Keep on this road, which turns into a stony track, and follow the yellow arrows on green through the scattered chalets of le Mary. Continue towards the next chalet, and just before you reach it, take the narrow path to the left, at a yellow arrow by a stone wall (15min).

The flowers on this walk are particularly abundant in springtime, especially trumpet gentians, several kinds of orchids, martagon lilies and alpenrose.

The path winds uphill through grassy meadows bright with flowers, and after about 10mins, at a post with a yellow arrow, bears left into the trees. Just before the col the path goes through an attractive dell where there are lots of orchids, tall yellow gentians and white daisies. ▶ When you reach the signpost at **Col de Cordon** (1636m), you can see both ways – back to the Mont Blanc massif and Col de Ramaz, and ahead to the mountains of the Vallée Verte, les Voirons and the Jura range on the horizon (45min).

Ahead on the left is the rocky pinnacle of the Pointe de Rovagne, 1795m.

Ignore the path bearing right and turn hard left on a narrow stony path which zigzags steeply down for about 10mins into a wide attractive valley with farms and grazing cows. Just before the farm at **Charmettes d'en Bas**

(1549m), you reach a jeep track at a signpost where you turn right and go up the jeep track to reach the chalets of **Charmettes d'en Haut** (1620m) (1hr 5min).

> This is **marmot** country, and if you keep quiet you may well see one of these furry creatures running across the rocks. Listen for the piercing whistle which is uttered by the marmot who is acting as sentry to warn the others that danger is approaching.

Go past the chalets and, at the next corner, you can either take the narrow, grassy path to the right, or stay on the jeep track, to reach the next col. You can already see a signpost on the skyline, so make for this landmark. ◄ Eventually you meet up with the jeep track and reach the signpost headed 'Alt. 1660m' ❶ (1hr 15min).

There are lots of orchids here, including common spotted, fragrant and black vanilla.

Do not go straight on through the gate, which seems the obvious way to go, but turn right, following the signs to Col de Chavannais/Col de Chavan/Haute Pointe. This is a narrow, grassy track which curls back the way you came but higher, and is marked with red/yellow splashes. The path goes very steeply up the side of the mountain, through slopes of flowers. After about 20mins you reach a ridge with a steep drop on your left. ◄ Continue along the top of the ridge to the **Col de Chavannais** (1800m), and go on to the signpost, about 10m down the other side ❷ (1hr 45min).

If you look back you have a good view of the Môle, which stands out in splendid isolation, and the Haute Pointe is on your right.

At the signpost do not go right, following the signs to Col de Chavan/Haute Pointe/Sommand, as this is a difficult, rocky path across scree slopes, where the snow lingers. Go left, following the signs to Chalet de Chavan/la Chèvrerie, down a stony path, marked by yellow splashes. There is a short section on scree, so watch your feet, but the path loses height rapidly to reach grass and small bushes. After about 30mins you come to a fork where the left path comes up from the Chalet de Chavan (this is not signed, so look out for it). Take the right fork and follow the yellow and then red/yellow markings steeply uphill to the signpost at the **Col de Chavan** (1757m) ❸ (2hr 45min). ◄

You might meet a flock of sheep here guarded by a large white pastous dog.

A chalet below the Haute Pointe

Follow the sign up to the **Haute Pointe**, which says 40min. The path is marked with intermittent blue splashes and is steep and stony at first. It then goes through a meadow with sheep, ending with a scramble up the rocks to the summit where there is a cross (3hr 25min).

The view from the **summit of the Haute Pointe** is spectacular. Starting from the west you can see Lake Geneva, the Jura and the Salève; the Pointe de Miribel, the Hirmentaz ridge and the Voirons in the Vallée Verte; the Grand Rocher de Nifflon and Pointe de la Gay near the village of Bellevaux, with the Dent d'Oche in the background; the Pointe de Chalune with the Roc d'Enfer behind; the Pointe d'Uble and the cross of the Pointe de Marcelly dominating Taninges; and finally the lone Môle peak. On the southern skyline are Mont Blanc and the higher Alpine peaks.

Walking back down to Sommand

The farm produces meat and milk for a dairy making Reblochon cheese.

Return by the same route to the **Col de Chavan** ❸ (3hr 45min) and follow the sign to Chalet du Coin/Sommand down the grassy hillside to the big farmhouse of **le Coin** at the start of a jeep track. ◄ Walk down the jeep track past another farm to reach the main road going from Sommand to Praz de Lys, and cross this to join another smaller road going steeply down through some attractive chalets to reach a cross. Turn left, still on the road, to the large parking area and the hotel where your car is parked in **Sommand** (4hr 45min).

WALK 17

Pointe d'Uble

Start/Finish	Near Bonnavaz, 1220m
Distance	10km
Total ascent	785m
Grade	Medium
Time	5hr
Maximum altitude	1965m
Map	IGN 3429 25 Bonneville/Cluses 1:25,000
Access	From St Jeoire, take the D907 to Taninges and then the D902 towards les Gets, and at le Pont des Gets turn left on the D328 towards Praz de Lys. Continue on the D328 through Bonnavaz for about 1km to les Plattes where you park opposite a farm.
Signposting	Good – new signposts and posts with yellow arrows on green

Although the start of this walk is along roads, once you get higher you are in attractive pastureland, with lovely meadow flowers in springtime and slopes of early purple and common spotted orchids higher up. In autumn the woods are full of interesting fungi, including the large red variety with white spots. From the summit ridge there is an unforgettable panorama of the surrounding peaks, especially of the nearby Roc d'Enfer, one of the most impressive mountains in this area.

From the signpost at les Plattes, walk down the D328 which you drove up. Shortly after you pass the hamlet of **Bonnavaz** on the right, where there is an attractive little chapel with a huge golden weather vane in the shape of a cockerel, and an imposing wooden door. The road crosses the **Ruisseau de Boutigny** which rushes attractively over boulders before joining the **River Foron**, and the meadows at the side of the road are carpeted with flowers. After about 20mins you reach a crossroads.

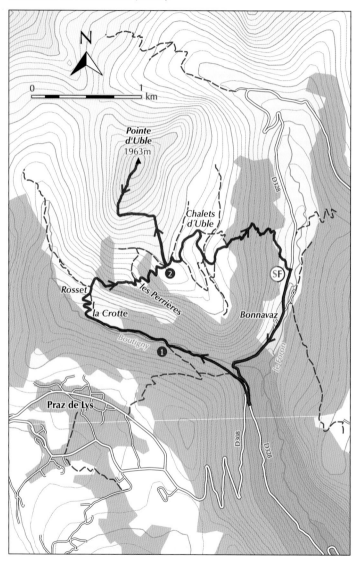

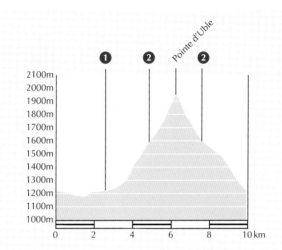

Turn right on the **D308** towards Praz de Lys and after about 100 metres, on a hairpin bend, take the narrower road which goes straight on towards la Crotte. You are walking along an attractive, narrow wooded valley with

A barn at la Crotte below the Pointe d'Uble: photo Sharon Bryand

the Boutigny stream rushing down on the right in a ravine and a wooded hill up on the left. After 10mins the road levels with the stream and becomes flat and easy. You pass a signpost on the left, headed 'Pont de la Crotte – alt. 1200m' **❶**, before crossing over a bridge into coniferous trees, where you will find a variety of fungi growing in the autumn. You reach a large wooden barn on the right and a signpost at **la Crotte** (1235m) (50min). The road walking is now over.

Leaving the road, which continues on as a jeep track, take the wide path up to the right, signposted 'Pointe d'Uble/les Munes'. Continue on the path, which becomes narrower and is bordered by pines. A few minutes later you come into open meadowland and zigzag up to reach the chalets of **Rosset** (1hr).

Go straight past the three chalets and follow the signs up to Pointe d'Uble. Continue on the rocky path which then bears to the right to pass two large troughs, going upwards round the contour of the slope through coniferous trees. You go through a wooden barrier and out into attractive meadowland, passing the ruins of **les Perrières**, which are almost completely hidden, to reach a post with a yellow arrow on green.

Go up to the left, ignoring a path off to the right and, a few minutes later, bear right at a further post with a yellow arrow. The path zigzags up through another patch of coniferous forest and then comes out again into open meadowland, continuing upwards to reach a humpy ridge where there is a wooden board saying 'Alpage d'Uble', and a signpost headed 'Alt. 1600m' **❷** (2hr 10min). ◀

Ahead you can see Mont Chéry, the top of the ski complex above les Gets, and the jagged peaks of the Roc d'Enfer to the left.

Go left following the sign Pointe d'Uble 1hr (straight on goes to Bonnavaz, which you will take on your return). You are now climbing steeply up to the summit of the mountain over open pastureland on a narrow path, which winds over to the left then right. The terrain suggests that the pointe will be another grassy hump, but in fact you come on to a ridge, the ground dropping away in front very abruptly, which is unexpected. This is the top of the **Pointe d'Uble** (1963m) (3hr 15min).

Looking down the Vallée de l'Arve from the Point d'Uble: photo Sharon Bryand

From the **Pointe d'Uble** you can see the Roc d'Enfer straight ahead, with the Pointe de Chalune to the left and the Haute Pointe behind. Below to your left is the Lac de Roy and the Pointe de Marcelly above Praz de Lys, while behind you to the south is the Vallée de l'Arve. If you walk to the end of the ridge, which takes five minutes, you will appreciate the sudden dramatic drop.

Retrace your steps to the board saying 'Alpage d'Uble' ❷, and turn left, following the sign to Bonnavaz. You can see the **Chalets d'Uble** below, but you never actually reach them. The track goes down, passing a small wooden chalet on the right. Go behind the chalet through a wooden barrier, and follow the grassy jeep track, which takes you down to the forest. At a T-junction go right (left goes to the Chalets d'Uble) and keep on the wide, grassy path until you meet a wider track (4hr 25min).

View of Praz de Lys and the Marcelly ridge from Pointe d'Uble: Photo Sharon Bryand

Turn down left and shortly after the path becomes a wide jeep track. You go through a wooden turnstile and into coniferous woods. After about 30mins of winding down through the woods, you reach the road at les Plattes and your car (5hr).

PRE-ALPES DU LEMAN

Dramatic view from above the Refuge de la Dent d'Oche (Walk 20): photo William Westermeyer

The rocky limestone mountains of the Pré-Alpes du Léman are the closest to the southern shore of Lake Geneva, and rise steeply from the fertile coastal plain behind Thonon-les-Bains and Evian-les-Bains. Their summits give dazzling views of the lake and the Swiss towns of Vevey and Montreux on the opposite shore, with the long straight line of the Jura mountains on the skyline, and to the east the high peaks in the Swiss cantons of Vaud and Valais. Two long-distance GR footpaths run through this area: the Balcon du Léman and the GR5, the main branch of which starts on the lake at St Gingolph, with an alternative start at Thonon-les-Bains,

and runs south through these mountains into the Val d'Abondance and Val de Morzine, from where it continues to Chamonix and on to the Mediterranean coast near Nice.

All the walks are within easy reach of both Evian, well known for its popular brand of mineral water, and the busier Thonon, historic capital of the Chablais. They are attractive spa towns where people come for health cures, so there is plenty of accommodation in hotels as well as campsites along the lake. Evian is an especially pleasant place to wander round, with beautiful gardens along the lakeshore and an internationally famous casino. Another obvious attraction of both

Passing the Dent d'Oche (Walk 19)

towns is the boat trips round the lake, getting off and on where you fancy on the French or the Swiss side, with the possibility of a visit to the famous Château de Chillon near Montreux.

A little set back from the lake is the small ski resort of Thollon-les-Mémises, with the Pic des Mémises rising above it, a dramatic viewpoint from where you can see the whole of Lake Geneva and mountains in all directions. Accessible by cable car in just five minutes, it is a popular spot for paragliders, who drift down over the blue waters of the lake. But there is a lovely walk up it too, through alpine pastures full of flowers. You will meet fewer people on the nearby Pic Boré, which is wilder and more secluded, but with equally spectacular views over the lake and of the nearby Dent d'Oche. The Dent d'Oche is the most well-known mountain of the three, its jagged twin peaks visible from miles away, with a refuge just below its summit. Despite the difficulty of the ascent and descent, this is a popular walk where you will always meet others, and you stand a good chance of seeing ibex on its rocky slopes.

The driving directions for walks in this section are from Evian-les-Bains.

WALK 18

Pic des Mémises

Start/Finish	Thollon Station, 1010m
Distance	11km
Total ascent	780m
Grade	Medium
Time	4hr 45min
Maximum altitude	1675m
Map	IGN 3528 ET Morzine Massif du Chablais 1:25,000
Access	From Evian, take the D24 to Thollon-les-Mémises and continue through the village, following signs to 'Station'. You pass the small hamlets of le Nouay and Chez les Aires to arrive at Thollon Station, a typical purpose-built ski resort where the cable car starts. Leave your car in the large car park on the left.
Signposting	Mostly good – new signposts, posts with yellow arrows on green, green arrows and red/white GR signs for the Balcon du Léman between the Col de Pertuis and the top of the cable car

This walk has outstanding views, as the Mémises ridge is the first high mountain south of Lake Geneva. You can see right across the lake to the Jura and Vaudois mountain ranges as far as the Bernese Oberland, and back to the main peaks of the Chablais. Both the ascent and descent have steep sections, but the walk along the ridge is a delight, and if you want to save your knees nearly 600m of descent, you can always take the cable car down to Thollon Station (open every day in July and August, and at weekends and on Wednesdays in June and September).

At the top of the car park there is an information board showing all the walks in the area, and a signpost headed 'Thollon les Mémises (Station)'. Following the signs to le Nouay/Chez les Aires, walk back down through the car park, in the direction you drove up, to another signpost at

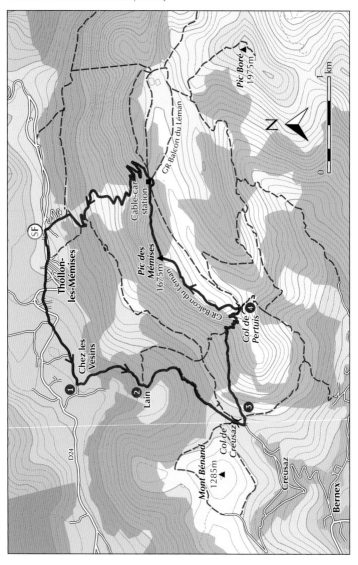

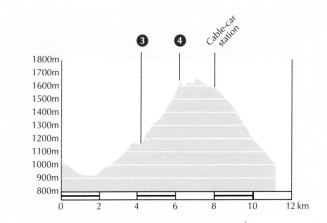

les Sapins. Continue down the road for about 100 metres, and where the road bends left, go straight on through a chain barrier and a no entry sign for cars (no sign here).

Pic des Mémises from Chez les Vesins

This leads into the original small hamlet of **Thollon-les-Mémises**, where there are older farm buildings and an exceptionally large stone trough on the right, which was the old village wash place. Continue down, passing the signpost 'Chez les Aires', and cross the D24 road at a post with a yellow arrow on green. Continue straight on to the signpost at le Nouay, cross the road again and turn left towards Chez les Vesins on a narrow road. You can see the small church at Thollon ahead. Continue along this road, passing a signpost headed 'Alt. 948m' and a Renault garage, to reach the hamlet of **Chez les Vesins** ❶ (25min).

Walk along to the small shrine and drinking fountain, next to which is a signpost. Following signs to Lain/Col de Creusaz, turn left and continue on as the tarmac road becomes a wide path. Follow the posts with yellow arrows on green – the path is stony but pleasant, going up through beech woods. Ignore all pathways branching off to reach a four-way junction and signpost at **Lain** ❷ (45min).

The track up to the left, signposted 'Col de Pertuis/Pic des Mémises', is a steeper way up, not much shorter and missing out the Col de Creusaz.

Follow the signs to Col de Creusaz/Bernex. ◀ Ignore all paths going off to the right or left and continue straight up through woodland on a wide track. At the end of the woods there is a post with a yellow arrow, and you come out into attractive open meadowland, carpeted with flowers in springtime. Continue across on a flat grassy path until you reach a large chalet and then a signpost at the **Col de Creusaz** (1165m) (1hr 30min).

Following signs to Creusaz, walk down a tarmac road for about 100 metres to the entrance of the car park and another signpost 'Col de Creusaz – alt. 1160m'. Bear left, following the signs to Col de Pertuis/Echelle/Pic des Mémises, to reach a turnstile ❸.

Leave the main wide track, which goes off to the right here, and keep straight ahead on a narrow path a grassy slope (there is no sign pointing up, so it is easy to miss). The path is well defined, climbing steeply up through open meadowland, with woods on the left. As you gain height, you get your first view of Lake Geneva down on your left. At a wide corner bearing right, do not continue on the main path but bear left into the forest on a narrow path, marked by a post with a yellow arrow, and continue until you reach a signpost headed 'Alt. 1380m' (2hr 10min). Following the signs to Col de Pertuis/Pic des Mémises, bear up right. ▶

The path left is where the steeper route from Lain rejoins.

> There are **explanatory posts** outlining details of the region (also in English) all along the Mémises ridge, and you shortly reach one of these about the Col de Pertuis. The path between here and the col is taken by cattle on their way to the higher pastures at the end of June each year, and back down again at the end of September (the barbed wire at the side of the path is for this reason). The board also indicates that the mountain starts here and, although the path is steep and stony, remember that it is not too steep for cows!

There are some blue and yellow splashes and some green arrows, but these are not needed as the way is obvious. The path zig-zags up, with a steep drop on one side and the impressive rock face of the Pic de Mémises on the other, and then winds round the side of the rock face to reach the **Col de Pertuis** (1512m) ❹ (2hr 40min). ▶

From the col you get your first breathtaking view of the mountains on the other side, dominated by the twin peaks of the nearby Dent d'Oche (2221m).

Turn left, following the sign to Pic des Mémises – you are now on the **GR Balcon du Léman**, indicated by red/white markings. The path climbs steeply up to the first peak, called Pertuis (1632m), where there is a post and a cairn (3hr). Now that the big climb is over this is a good place to stop for a picnic as further along you are likely to meet the crowds who have come up by cable car.

From Pertuis, carry on up along a wide ridge path to reach the highest point, the **Pic des Mémises** (1675m), which is marked with a cross, an electricity aerial and a map showing the surrounding peaks (3hr 20min).

> The mountain **views** on both sides are extensive. Nearest are the peaks of the Chablais, dominated by Pic Boré and the Dent d'Oche, while across the lake can be seen the mass of les Diablerets and

Lake Geneva and the Swiss shore from Pic des Mémises

the peaks of the Swiss Alps, with the Eiger, Mönch and Jungfrau just visible in the distance. Strung out below along the lakeshore are the towns of Lausanne, Vevey and Montreux.

Continue along the ridge towards the cable car station ('Télécabine gare supérieure'), past an information board entitled 'les Carrières' (the quarries), explaining that the quarries directly below were exploited from the end of the 18th century, producing the beautiful blue-grey stone used for many of the buildings of Geneva, Lausanne and Montreux. After passing two chalets you reach the **cable car station**, which also has a restaurant (3hr 30min). ◄

If you want to save your knees nearly 600m of descent, you can take the cable car down to Thollon Station.

Go to the signpost at the entrance to the cable car station and follow the signs to Thollon (station), not to Chalets des Mémises. This is a wide, stony track which winds down the mountain under the cable car on the track taken by skiers. It is an easy gradient, with obvious short cuts every so often. You come out on the road opposite the car park in **Thollon Station** (4hr 45min).

WALK 19
Pic Boré

Start/Finish	Les Chautets, near Bernex, 1100m
Distance	10km
Total ascent	885m
Grade	Strenuous
Time	5hr
Maximum altitude	1975m
Map	IGN 3528 ET Morzine Massif du Chablais 1:25,000
Access	From Evian, take the D21 towards St-Paul-en-Chablais and then the D52 to Bernex. At the entrance to Bernex do not turn down right, but carry on straight along a narrower road following signs to Pré Richard and an old wooden signpost to Trossy and Charmet. After Charmet you reach a bridge (Pont de Morgon) with a large café/restaurant on the right. Do not turn right to cross the bridge towards Pré Richard/Dent d'Oche, but carry straight on a smaller road (the walking signpost at the bridge indicates le Chon). Continue up this small road, past le Chon on the left, and park on the right by the signpost at les Chautets (Parking), 1100m.
Signposting	Good when lower down, with new signposts and red/white GR markings for the Balcon du Léman, but very few signs higher up, although most paths are well defined

Although this walk is fairly long, it is only the final scramble to the summit and the ridge walk afterwards that are challenging. The ridge is quite long and narrow, with a steep drop on one side, so tread very carefully, especially if you do not like exposure. The lower slopes of the mountain are pastureland for cows, full of lovely flowers in summer and even into autumn, and although there are some ski installations higher up, the dramatic views over Lake Geneva and the mountains of Vaud and the Valais offset this disadvantage.

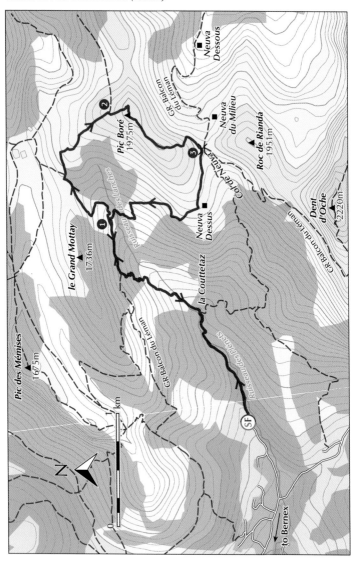

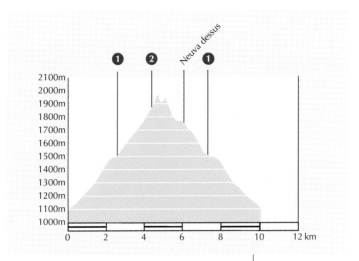

From the signpost 'les Chautets (Parking)', continue up the tarmac road towards la Couttetaz, with a stream on the right. The road soon becomes a stony jeep track, crossing the stream from time to time, and gains height very gradually. The stream is the **Ruisseau des Plénets**, which burbles away attractively, with a few small waterfalls coming down into it on the right. Continue up through the woods to reach a junction at the signpost at **la Couttetaz** (1247m) (30min).

Turn left towards Sur les Prés/Neuvaz Dessus (Neuvaz on the signposts is spelt Neuva on the maps), still on the stony jeep track, and cross the stream. The track crosses the stream again and bears to the left as you come out into open pastureland, with fir trees on the left. At a fork soon after you bear left again (no signs), and start to climb up the grassy slopes more steeply.

▶ As you get higher you can see the steep cliffs of **le Grand Mottay** towering above on the left before you enter the trees again and reach a signpost headed 'Alt. 1475m' (1hr 10min).

Even in autumn there are blue gentians still in flower, not the larger trumpet variety but the smaller fringed and field gentians, both with four petals instead of the usual five.

173

Turn right towards Neuvaz Dessus/Col de Neuvaz, still on a stony jeep track. You are now on a variant of the **GR Balcon du Léman**, marked by red/white signs, until the next signpost. This is a fairly flat path which contours along through the trees, with the cliffs of le Grand Mottay still on the left. Ahead you get your first view of Pic Boré, rearing up into the sky, and you may wonder how on earth you are going to get up there. After about 10mins you arrive at a fork at the next signpost, headed 'Alt. 1480m' ❶ (1hr 20min).

The signpost for the left turn, the way you want to go, is missing and there is only a VTT sign pointing up here. Take this turn, leaving the GR path which goes down right towards Neuvaz Dessus/Col de Neuvaz. ◀ The track becomes grassier as it winds up with the stream on the right and the cliffs on the left, and becomes even steeper before reaching the crest of the hill at a post with a small green sign at the top of the VTT track (2hr).

This is the way you will come from after going up to the summit and returning via the col.

Bear right and go under the Parchet chairlift, which comes up from the top of the Mémises cable car from Thollon, and then go under the Phébus ski-tow. You are now on a wide jeep track, which eventually goes to the Col de Parchet, but you very shortly leave this. When you are at the same height as the top of the ski-tow, take the narrow undefined path on the right which goes behind the top of the ski-tow, and make for the Parchet chairlift ahead. You are now on the grassy ski slope coming down from the top of the chairlift, with a fence on your right. Go up the ski slope until you reach the hut at the top ❷ (2hr 40min).

From here you can see the summit of Pic Boré directly ahead. Although it is only just over 100m higher, it is this last part which is more difficult, especially if you do not like exposure. Climb up the steep grassy slope which leads into a stony chimney in the rock face. You will need hands to scramble up this (a few orange splashes to guide you).

When you come out at the top, take care as there is a sheer drop in front of you down the other side.

The path is very exposed as it bears to the right for the final climb to the grassy hump, which is the **Pic Boré** itself, marked by a small cairn (3hr 10min).

Looking up at Pic Boré

> The summit of **Pic Boré** is a good spot to stop as you can see the entire lake, the towns and countryside of the Swiss shore, and the mountains of Vaud, the Valais and the Jura. Nearby are the rocky peaks of Grammont and les Jumelles, with the slopes of the Dent d'Oche dominating the view straight ahead.

Pick your way down from the top of the grassy hump and walk along the ridge. The path goes mainly to the left of the ridge, but it is very exposed with a steep drop down on the right – keep your eyes on the path if you do not like exposure. If you look back as you walk along, you have an impressive view of the grassy summit of the Pic Boré where you have been – it looks a long way up! The ridge is quite long, and at the end of it, at 1938m, there is a post and a fence.

Directly ahead is the imposing Dent d'Oche, and the path straight on is one of the ways to its summit.

From here the Col de Neuvaz, where you are heading, is directly below and the chalets of Neuvaz Dessus off to the right. Make your way down the steep slope, with the fence on your left, to reach the crossroads and signpost at **Col de Neuvaz** (1775m) ❸. Here you re-join the Balcon du Léman (3hr 40min). ◀

Turn right towards Neuvaz Dessus/Sur les Prés to reach the chalets of **Neuvaz Dessus**, now fallen into disrepair. After the chalets, the path bears to the right into the trees, and a few minutes later there is an old wooden signpost, with a red/white GR sign, indicating straight on to Sur les Prés/Bernex. The path contours round the side of the mountain, and you can see the grassy hump of Pic Boré and the Parchet chairlift straight ahead. It then starts to wind downhill, gradually losing height, to reach a post with a yellow arrow on green and a GR sign. Turn left, and continue down to reach the next post where you go straight. Continue descending to reach the signpost headed 'Alt. 1480m' where you turned off on the way up ❶ (4hr 20min).

Go left following the signs to Chalets de Sur les Prés and reverse your route up, passing the signpost headed 'Alt. 1475m', where you bear left, to reach the signpost at la Couttetaz. Here you turn right and walk down the jeep track to reach the parking area (5hr).

Peaks of the Chablais rising above a sea of clouds

WALK 20
Dent d'Oche

Start/Finish	La Fétiuère, near Bernex, 1230m
Distance	7.5km
Total ascent	960m
Grade	Difficult
Time	5hr 45min
Maximum altitude	2220m
Map	IGN 3528 ET Morzine/Massif du Chablais 1:25,000
Access	From Evian, take the D21 towards St-Paul-en-Chablais and then the D52 to Bernex. At the entrance to Bernex do not turn down right, but carry on straight along a narrower road following an old wooden signpost to Trossy/Charmet/Dent d'Oche. After Charmet you reach a bridge (Pont de Morgon), with a large café/restaurant on the right. Turn right towards Pré Richard/Dent d'Oche, and continue for about 2km till you come to a small parking area with the chalet (café in season) of la Fétiuère on the left.
Signposting	Adequate – new signposts, red/white GR signs for the Balcon du Léman and some yellow arrows

This walk is a wonderful experience, and from the summit are glorious views of Mont Blanc and across Lake Geneva to the peaks of the Valais and Bernese Oberland. However, the top is steep and exposed, with chains for protection in some places, so is not for anyone afraid of heights, although you can just go as far as the refuge and return the same way. The unusual shape of this mountain, which is really two distinct peaks, can be recognised from afar and resembles two spaced-out teeth, hence its name. This is a nature reserve, so keep a watch out for ibex as there is quite a colony here.

An **ascent of the Dent d'Oche** took much more organisation in the past, as shown by this account of a weekend trip in 1880. A group of Swiss Alpine

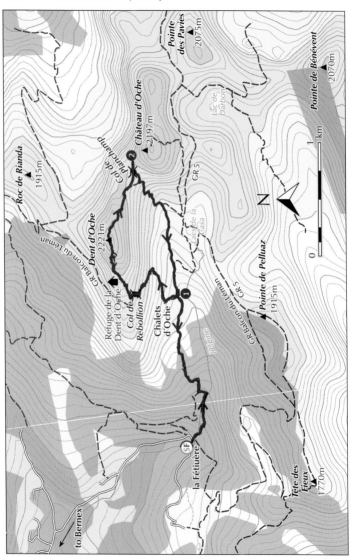

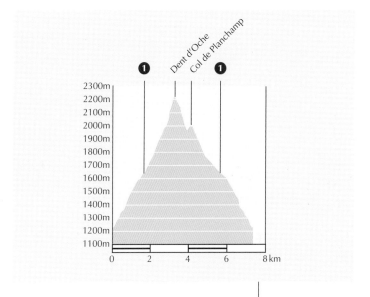

Club members took the paddle steamer from Geneva to Evian and then walked up to the higher chalet on the mountain for the night, a height gain of almost 2000m. They got up at 5.00am, and after reaching the summit two hours later, walked all the way back down to Evian, this time via the Chalets de Mémises, to catch the paddle steamer back home.

Follow the wooden signpost to Chalet/Dent d'Oche, which is next to a new signpost stating that this takes 3hrs. This is a wide rocky path, which goes steeply up through widely spaced woods with a stream on the left. In parts the path has curious rocky ridges and lots of tree roots which makes walking uncomfortable. You cross a wooden bridge called Pont des Bures, constructed in 2009 by the Lions Club in Thonon (30min).

After the bridge you are walking through alpine pasture with a magnificent view of the formidable looking

179

Dent d'Oche ahead, but do not be discouraged. It has an unusual formation – a rocky peak rearing up in front, the Château d'Oche, which sweeps down to a grassy ridge called the Col de Planchamp and then up the long rocky ridges of the Dent d'Oche itself.

Continue on this path, which climbs gently along the bottom of the mountain, past a low ruin with coniferous woods set back on the left, with the precipitous slopes of the Dent d'Oche behind. Re-cross the stream, which has now become a rivulet, and follow the path. On a grassy knoll up on the left is a wooden cross. After a climb of 400m, you reach the **Chalets d'Oche** (1630m) ❶ (1hr 20min).

> This is a **farm** where you can buy freshly made cheese and milk in summer, if the building is open. There is a notice on it telling walkers that they are in a nature reserve, and that dogs should be kept on a lead. Alongside is another building housing the flocks of sheep and goats to be seen on the surrounding slopes. Behind there is a magnificent view of Lake Geneva with the Jura on the skyline.

At the signpost just beyond the chalet, continue straight on towards Col de Rebollion/Refuge de la Dent d'Oche/Dent d'Oche. Here you join the **GR Balcon du Léman**, so look out for red/white markings. As the path goes up steeply you can see over on the right the narrow valley you will come back down and a beautiful high waterfall. The path bears to the right along the side of the mountain, as if you are making for the cleft between the two peaks, which is the Col de Planchamp. ◄ However, the track winds round to the left instead of continuing towards the ridge, where you can see two attractive little lakes on the other side, the Lacs de la Casa, one green and the other brown.

There is a dramatic view of the Château d'Oche ahead and, across the valley on the right, the grassy mountain ridge of the Pointe de Pelluaz with the silhouettes of two crosses.

At the **Col de Rebollion** (1915m) follow the signpost right to the Refuge de la Dent d'Oche/Dent d'Oche (2hr 20min). From here there is a magnificent view in front of Mont César and the Pic des Mémises ridge with the lake

beyond and Jura mountains on the horizon, and the serrated crest of Pic Boré to the right.

Continue on the steep path towards the Refuge de la Dent d'Oche. It forks left round two jutting-out rocks at a yellow paint sign saying 'Refuge 15mins'where you can see chains snaking up to the refuge above (do not go right on a steep scree slope). This is the start of a steep scramble up a rocky chimney where there are three sets of chains to help, but be extra careful in wet weather when the rocks are slippery. Follow the yellow arrows up to the **Refuge de la Dent d'Oche**, which you can see as you scramble up. It is perched in a dramatic position on a rocky mound at 2113m (3hr).

The Refuge de la Dent d'Oche, **www.refuge ladentdoche.ffcam.fr**, owned by the French Alpine Club, has dormitory accommodation for 76 people, and provides meals. It is open in July and August, weekends only June and September.

Rocky ascent of the Dent d'Oche: photo Richard Saynor

181

Negotiating chains on the Dent d'Oche

If you have found the going difficult up to the refuge, you should retrace your steps, as the way ahead is steep and exposed.

Continue on the path going round and up the mountain at the back of the refuge. At a fork keep left (right is more difficult) to reach an airy ridge. You go over this to traverse along the other side of the ridge before another steep scramble over rocks following yellow arrows – you need to use both hands, but there are cables provided, which is a great help. You climb onto a rocky shoulder – this is rather exposed but not as bad as it looks from below. Continue along this ridge to an iron cross dated 1981 (blessed in September 1982). From the cross it is a few minutes to the real summit of the **Dent d'Oche** (2221m) where there is a cairn (3hr 20min).

From the **summit** the views in all directions are breathtaking, not only of the nearby Cornettes de Bise but of Mont Blanc and as far as the Eiger, Mönch and Jungfrau in the Bernese Oberland.

The descent from the summit to the Col de Planchamp is difficult and very exposed, with a sign saying 'Passage aerien' – you may prefer to return the way you came up.

Be very careful as you pick your way down as this is the north side and snow hangs around late in the season. There is another helpful chain in one place as you continue to negotiate the steep rocky slope, watching carefully for the yellow splashes which indicate the easier way. After about 40mins you reach an imposing expanse of flat rock where there is a 20-metre cable for support as you feel your way across. This is not easy, with a steep drop, but there are numerous footholds.

A few minutes later you come to the last chain, where you climb in and over a rocky gully and continue along the edge of the mountain, passing a signpost indicating Chalets d'Oche par le Col de Planchamp (4hr). ▶ Along here you can see the path below and there is an obvious steep short cut, but it is better to continue to the **Col de Planchamp** ❷ (1998m), which is a lovely wide grassy pass (4hr 20min). This is where you meet the sign saying 'Passage aerien' indicating that the way you have come down is exposed!

You will often see ibex in this section.

From both sides of the **Col de Planchamp** there are magnificent views. To the north the valley drops down to the village of Novel with Lake Geneva beyond. You can see Montreux and the motorway on the other side of the lake, with the Vaudois Alps in the background. Behind is the imposing high rock face of the Château d'Oche with an intriguing cave opening at the bottom, just too far up to reach.

At the col continue down the path into the top end of the valley towards the Chalets d'Oche, which you can see in front. ▶ At the bottom of the valley follow the signpost headed 'Alt. 1670m' towards Chalets d'Oche, now only a few minutes away. The path undulates pleasantly

Look out for more ibex and marmots as you descend this path.

Heading down from the Col de Planchamp towards an Ibex: photo Richard Saynor

through the valley and is a welcome relief after all the climbing and scrambling you have done. You pass a further sign, where the path left goes to Lacs de la Casa/ Lac de Darbon, before reaching the **Chalets d'Oche** at ❶ (5hr).

From here, retrace your steps to the *buvette* at **la Fétiuère** (5hr 45min).

VAL D'ABONDANCE

Val d'Abondance from the Pas de la Bosse (Walk 21): photo Richard Saynor

The Val d'Abondance lies to the south of the Pré-Alpes du Léman, and follows the main tributary of the River Dranse. It is a land of plenty, as the name implies, and origin of the distinctive brown and white Abondance cows which are renowned for the excellent cheese made from their milk. Crossbred from Swiss and local species, the cattle became a recognised breed in 1894 and can now be found all over the Haute Savoie. The farmers are very proud of their individual cows, and there are annual contests to select the 'queen of the herd'.

Farming is still very much a way of life here, and the farms in the valley are built of wood in the traditional style, with intricately carved balconies, some with their original roofs made either of locally quarried slate or fir-wood tiles, called *tavaillons*. The living quarters face south and hay is stacked under the roof in enormous lofts. In the past large extended families lived together, the grown-up sons bringing their wives into the family home. Small chapels were often built on summer pastures for masses to be held to bless the flocks, and in some places these are still held, such

Cornettes de Bise from the Pointe des Mattes (Walk 26)

as at the chapel at Ubine on the walk around Mont Chauffé.

Since the 1950s life in the valley has changed considerably as tourism and skiing have become the main source of income. The valley is now connected to the Portes du Soleil skiing area, one of the most extensive in the Alps, linking eight resorts in France and four in Switzerland, with more than 200 ski lifts. However, despite the building of apartments and hotels to house the influx of tourists, much of the valley has remained unspoiled and retains its charm and tranquillity, especially in the summer.

This is a popular area for walking, and the GR5 long-distance footpath runs through on its way south to Nice. Some of the loveliest walks in the Haute Savoie are here, although many are higher and more challenging than those in other sections. The most difficult of all is the formidable Cornettes de Bise, which dominates the entire valley, and at 2432m is its highest peak. There are various routes to its summit, some on part of the GR5, others from across the border in Switzerland.

Driving up the valley, the first village you reach is its *chef-lieu*, Abondance. It is an attractive place, which has been less affected by the ski boom than the villages higher up. In the centre is the old abbey, founded in 1080 by monks from the nearby St Maurice in Switzerland. This is one of the few abbeys in the Haute Savoie that is still intact, and you can visit its church, cloisters with 15th-century frescoes and museum. Above Abondance are several small lakes that drain into streams which feed the River Dranse, and the Lac de Tavaneuse and the Lac d'Arvouin are both popular destinations for walks.

Further up, in the sunniest spot in the valley, is the smaller village of Chapelle d'Abondance, which was the first to be inhabited. It has an unusual church, with a steeple of three onion-shaped domes that the inhabitants are very proud of. The first inn was opened in the village in 1894, and in 1925 this was transformed into a hotel, the prestigious Les Cornettes, which is still owned by the same family. Also dominated by the Cornettes de Bise, the beautiful walk around Mont Chauffé starts from here.

Châtel is the last village in the valley before you go over the Pas de Morgins into Switzerland, and in the Middle Ages there was a castle here to guard the pass, origin of the name Châtel. Originally the poorest of the three communities due to its higher altitude and less fertile pastureland, the inhabitants compensated with a lucrative smuggling trade. Just outside the village is la Vieille Douane, a museum of smuggling with fascinating information on how the wily peasants were able to outwit the customs men (called *gabelous* in local dialect), and the walk up to the Pic de Morclan on the Swiss border follows one of the smugglers' routes. Châtel was also known for its slate mines, which were worked in the winter months when the fields were under snow, the last one closing as recently as 1986.

Châtel opened its first ski lift in 1947, and smuggling died a natural death once it was realised that more money was to be made from winter sports. It is now the most prosperous of the three villages, and is a major crossroads in the Portes du Soleil skiing complex. Fortunately for walkers, the two high peaks of Pointe des Mattes and Mont de Grange, the second highest in the valley, are on the opposite side of the valley from the lifts, and Mont de Grange is now a nature reserve where moufflon were introduced in 1969.

The driving directions for walks in this section are from Abondance.

WALK 21
Cornettes de Bise

Start/Finish	Chalets de Bise, 1495m
Alternative finish	Chevenne, 1220m
Distance	12.5km; or 11.5km
Total ascent	1235m
Total descent	1235m; or 1370m
Grade	Difficult
Time	7hr 15min; or 6hr 45min
Maximum altitude	2430m
Map	IGN 3528 ET Morzine Massif du Chablais 1:25,000
Access	From Abondance, take the D22 towards Thonon-les-Bains and at Vacheresse turn right following the signs to Site de Bise. Drive for about 10km to the end of the road and park in the large space by the Chalets de Bise, where there is an information board with a map of walks in the area.
Signposting	Mostly good – French and Swiss signposts, red/white markings on the rocks and some faded red chamois heads higher up
Note	The alternative finish is less demanding at the end of a long day. However, you must leave a second car at the Chevenne parking, to the north of Chapelle d'Abondance.

The Cornettes de Bise (meaning 'horns of cold wind') is one of the highest peaks in the Chablais and can be seen for miles around. The view from the summit is breathtaking, and ibex are frequently seen. It is a popular hike in summer, with several trails leading to the summit from both sides of the French-Swiss border, some easier than others.

The route described here makes a wonderful outing, going all the way round the mountain as well as up it, and avoiding the difficult and exposed Couloir de Serrauquin. However, it is long and challenging, with some decidedly airy parts, and should only be attempted by experienced walkers who are prepared to make a very early start. It is advisable to wait until a fine day in midsummer before tackling the walk, as snow can linger on the rocks higher up, and the north facing slopes of the Pas de Chaudin can be treacherous if covered in snow or ice.

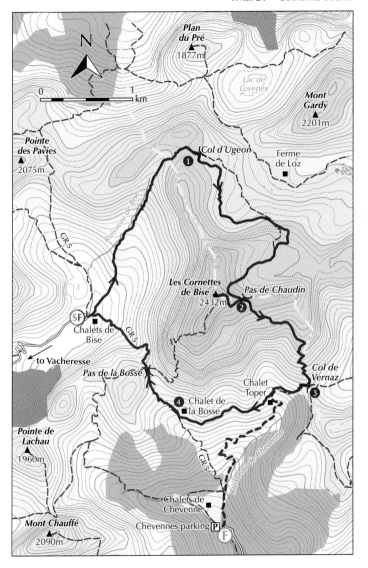

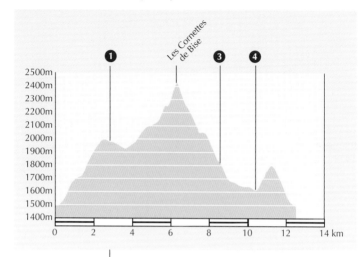

The **Site de Bise** at the start of the walk is a lovely spot with a café, a farm with goats milling around (where you can buy cheese) and a museum of local life. One of the buildings here is the Refuge de Bise, which recently closed for renovation and will probably not re-open until 2018 at the earliest.

Ibex family below summit: photo Philip Jenkins

When it does, an alternative to doing the walk in one very long day would be to start at the large parking area in Chevenne and walk up to the Pas de la Bosse and then down to the Refuge de Bise for an overnight. Then on the second day, follow the route as described here, but from the Col de Vernaz on the descent, continue down to Chevenne instead of crossing over by the Chalet Toper.

From the Chalets de Bise walk up to the signpost next to the refuge, and follow the signs to Pas de la Bosse/Col d'Ugeon. Just after the museum of local life on the left, with farm implements in the garden, you reach another signpost, where you bear left towards Col d'Ugeon. This is a narrow path, which can be a little slippery when wet, winding up over grassy pastures, full of flowers in summer. ▶ The **Ruisseau de Bise** soon comes in on the left, and the path continues up to reach the French-Swiss border just before the **Col d'Ugeon** (1964m) ❶ (1hr 45min).

Look out for alpenrose, gentians, pulsatilla anemones and the rare yellow bellflower (*campanula thyrsoides*).

You are now in Switzerland until the Col de Vernaz (Col de Verne on the Swiss signposts), so the signposts are the yellow Swiss ones. Follow the path to Montagne de Loz/Taney, contouring east and then south across grassy slopes, staying at about the same height. After about 15mins you pass a small mountain lake with a weather station mast beside it. The path here is not too well marked, although there are occasional red/white signs on the rocks, and you stay at about the same height. Quite a long way down below on the left you can see the long, low buildings of the Ferme de Loz.

At the next signpost (2hr 20min), follow the signs to Cornettes de Bise. The path turns to the southwest and becomes rocky and steeper, going up through a boulder field and past snow patches, even in high summer. At the **Pas de Chaudin** (2250m) ❷ there is another yellow Swiss signpost pointing up right to the Cornettes de Bise. (Do not confuse the Pas de Chaudin with the Col de Chaudin, which is further east.) Straight on down leads to the Col de Vernaz, which is the path you take on your return from the summit (3hr). ▶

There are a lot of ibex on the rocks here, which do not seem to be at all afraid of walkers.

Cornettes de Bise in early autumn: photo Richard Saynor

Follow the signs up to the **Cornettes de Bise** on a steep, rocky path.

The path up to the Cornettes de Bise should not be attempted if there is snow or ice on the rocks.

You should watch your step, a sobering reminder being the plaque you pass commemorating Gérard Hirt, a young man who fell to his death in August 1962, aged only 19 years.

There are a number of diverging paths in between the rocks, probably made by chamois and hundreds of previous walkers, but try to follow the official one with red/white markings and a few painted chamois heads, now somewhat faded. Although this path is steep, it is not technically difficult or too airy. ◀ The path climbs round the shoulder of the mountain to the right, and you eventually see the cross on the summit above you. Continue up and then bear sharp left for the final ascent to the summit, where there is a boundary cairn (4hr).

*Roc de Chaudin and
Pas de Chaudin:
photo Richard Saynor*

The **Cornettes de Bise** is one of the highest and
most dramatic of the Chablais peaks so the panorama is exceptional. On a clear day you can see
Mont Blanc due south, with the peaks of the Dents
du Midi on the left and further left still the Grand
Combin. To the north is Lake Geneva with the town
of Vevey on the opposite shore, and the long line
of the Jura mountains in the background. Nearer
are all the high peaks of the Chablais, including the
Dent d'Oche, Mont de Grange and Mont Chauffée.

To return, take the same path you took up, bearing
left down the steep rocky shoulder of the mountain to
reach the Pas de Chaudin and the yellow Swiss signpost
❷ (4hr 30min).
Continue straight on following the sign to the Col de
Verne/Vernaz, round the bottom of the Roc de Chaudin.
There is a further rocky descent and then a grassy path.
Where it divides, take the lower path, which brings you to

the two wooden buildings of la Caliaz (2067m), perched on the bare hillside (5hr). These are the highest chalets in the Chablais, and were completely renovated in 1985 when one of them was equipped as an emergency refuge.

From here you can see the col below you, and the path zigzags down on a steep and stony path to the sign-posts at the **Col de Vernaz/Verne** (1815m) ❸ (5hr 30min). Take the path to the right towards Chalets de Chevenne, which is steep and rather eroded, to reach the jeep track on the right leading to the Chalet Toper.

Alternative finish at Chevenne

If you have left a second car at the large parking area above Chevenne (see Access for Walk 22), keep on the wide jeep track, following the signs to Chalets de Chevenne. After about 1hr the GR5 joins your path from the right at a signpost **Chalets de Chevenne** (1280m) and a few minutes later you arrive at the parking area (6hr 45min).

To finish at the Chalets de Bise, turn right and walk along past the **Chalet Toper**, and soon you pass a small wooden shrine. Contour straight across the slope in a westerly direction towards the ruins of the Chalet de la Bosse. Initially this path is an old cart track, but it soon deterio-rates into a narrow path and almost disappears. Traverse the grassy slope, keeping to the same altitude, and take care not to slip if the grass is wet. If you get too low, you will have to climb up again. You join the GR5 at the ruins of the **Chalet de la Bosse** ❹ (6hr 30min).

Turn right and follow the red/white markings up to the **Pas de la Bosse** (1816m), an unwelcome ascent. From here it is all downhill, across grassy slopes, bright with gentians and pulsatilla anemones in early summer, back to the **Chalets de Bise** (7hr 15min).

WALK 22
Lac d'Arvouin

Start/Finish	Chevenne, Chapelle d'Abondance, 1220m
Distance	10.5km
Total ascent	725m
Grade	Medium
Time	4hr 45min
Maximum altitude	1850m
Map	IGN 3528 ET Morzine Massif du Chablais 1:25,000
Access	From Abondance, take the D22 to Chapelle d'Abondance, and in the centre of the village, turn left just before the Hôtel Montfleury (there is no sign, but if you miss it take the following left turn). Go up this narrow road for about 2km to the large parking area at Chevenne.
Signposting	Good – new signposts and posts with yellow arrows on green

This walk is in one of the loveliest areas of the Haute Savoie, and gives impressive views of the three highest peaks of the Val d'Abondance: the Cornettes de Bise, Mont de Grange and Mont Chauffé. It is best done in late spring or early summer, after the snow has melted and the paths have dried out, and when there is an abundance of flowers – bright blue trumpet gentians, golden yellow globeflowers, white pasque flowers and several different species of orchids. You might also see marmots, chamois or ibex, re-introduced in the 1950s.

▶ From the parking area, turn left and walk down the road for about 300 metres to reach a signpost headed 'Alt. 1180m' and turn left again on the Chemin de Blanchet towards la Côte/Bonnatrait. This is a pleasant, flattish track through woods on a *sentier découverte*, with several small information boards and a panoramic map of Mont de Grange, which you see ahead. After about 15mins you join a jeep track where you turn right and wind down to reach a tarmac road. Turn left, following the sign to Chez

There is a large wooden shelter by the parking area with a map and information boards on the geological features of the area, and the animals and plants you might see.

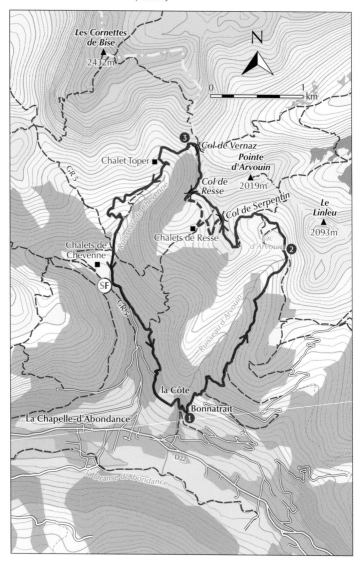

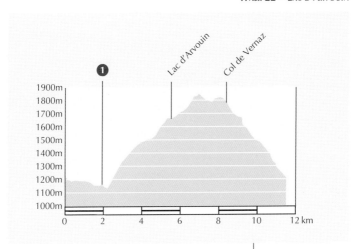

les Thoules/Chapelle d'Abondance, winding round the hill with a few chalets dotted about. ▶ You reach **la Côte** (1155m) where there is a signpost and a large chalet on the left called 'Haute Cime'. Opposite is an information board on the geological history of the valley. Following the sign to Bonnatrait/Chapelle d'Abondance, take a grassy path behind an older chalet called 'la Côte'. The path goes slightly down through woods and over a stream (30min).

Ahead is a glorious view of the Dents du Midi, and on the right you can see down into the Val d'Abondance and the village of Chapelle d'Abondance.

Looking down on Chapelle d'Abondance from la Côte

There is a board here on the **Mystère d'eau** (the mystery of water), explaining that this stream was originally thought to flow from the Lac d'Arvouin, but now it seems that the outlet of the lake is not known.

About 150 metres beyond the stream, at a signpost at **Bonnatrait ❶**, turn up left. There is no sign pointing up this narrow path, but as you go higher, there are a few posts with yellow arrows on green. The path goes steeply up to reach a T-junction where you turn right and continue through coniferous woods. At a little chalet on the right and another post with a yellow arrow, continue very steeply upwards through the forest to reach a signpost headed 'Bonnatrait – alt. 1250m'. Turn left towards Lac d'Arvouin/Col de Vernaz, crossing the end of a jeep track where there is a parking area and another signpost. Follow the sign to Lac d'Arvouin up the steep path to reach a stony jeep track (1hr).

On the left there is a beautiful view of nearby Mont Chauffé.

Turn left and continue on this jeep track through woodland until an intersection with a signpost. Turn right, following signs to Lac d'Arvouin. Continue upwards, through widely spaced coniferous trees, steeply at first and then flattening out before rising again. ◄

You reach a four-way junction at a signpost headed 'Alt. 1442m' (1hr 25min). Following signs to Lac d'Arvouin/Col de Vernaz, continue upwards on a track along the side of a valley with the **Ruisseau d'Arvouin** on the left. Go through a wooden gate where you enter an alpine pasture called Alpage des Chèvres and pass a chalet called 'la Maisonette' on the left. There are a lot of goats here, grazing in an attractive deep bowl in the mountains.

In spring the slopes here are white with narcissus-flowered anemones, and you'll see lots of spring gentians, globe flowers and early purple orchids.

The path goes up round the right side of the bowl, with occasional yellow arrows on green, and goes through a gate at the end of the pasture. ◄ The path winds around and crosses some rocky scree before cresting the top of the slope by a small stream to reveal the **Lac d'Arvouin** (1663m) in front of you ❷ (2hr 15min).

Lac d'Arvouin

The **Lac d'Arvouin** is a typical alpine lake surrounded by mountains, round and deep green, its shores fringed by reeds and bright yellow marsh marigolds. For seven or eight months a year it is covered with ice, but in summer it is a paradise for brown trout and minnows.

Follow the signs to Col de Serpentin/Chalets de Chevenne (the path merging from the right comes from Sevan) on a path going round the right side of the lake and curling up the mountain. You pass two large barns called the Chalets d'Arvouin, which have been restored, where there is a beautiful view overlooking the lake with the peak of **Le Linleu** (2093m) rearing up beyond (2hr 40min).

Follow the signs to Col de Serpentin/Col de Vernaz/Chalets de Chevenne, bearing left up the slope to reach the top of the ridge at a signpost 'Tête de l'Avalanche – alt. 1854m', the highest point of the walk – the actual peak is up to the left (3hr 5min). Turn right along the ridge

There is an easier route going down about 80m to the Chalets de Resse and back up to the Col de Resse. It takes about 15mins longer, but avoids the section with chains.

to reach the **Col de Serpentin** (1832m), a perfect rest spot with glorious views.

From the col take the path to the left which curls round the hill along a path which is easy at first, but then has a short tricky section protected with chains where you pick your way down over the rocks. ◄

At the **Col de Resse** (1781m) there is a signpost and an even closer view of the Cornettes de Bise (3hr 25min). Turn right towards the Col de Vernaz/Chevenne on a narrow path which goes round the side of the mountain and up to the **Col de Vernaz** (1815m) ❺ (3hr 40min).

Here you are on the Swiss border and there is a yellow signpost down to the right saying Verne/Taney. (The French signpost calls this the Col de Vernaz, 1815m, whereas the Swiss one calls it the Col de Verne, 1814m.) To the right is the Rhône valley and ahead the towering Cornettes de Bise, where you might see walkers toiling up to the summit, and a refuge on the slope of the mountain. Take the path down to the left signed 'Chalets de Chevenne'. This is steep in places as there is a lot of erosion. You shortly reach a jeep track going to the **Chalet Toper** up on the right, where there are horses, cows and sheep grazing. Turn down to the left and continue down the wide track, which is mostly in the open with little shade.

After about 1hr the GR5 joins your path from the right at a signpost at **Chalets de Chevenne** (1280m) and a few minutes later you arrive back at the parking area (4hr 45min).

WALK 23

Autour du Mont Chauffé

Start/Finish	Le Sauvage, Abondance, 1235m
Distance	11.5km
Total ascent	870m
Grade	Strenuous
Time	4hr 50min
Maximum altitude	1685m
Map	IGN 3528 ET Morzine/Massifs du Chablais 1:25,000
Access	From Abondance, drive through the village, and just as you leave it, take the small road hard left indicating le Mont. Go through le Mont to reach a T-junction where you turn right towards le Sauvage and continue to the parking on the left by an information board and a signpost (3km from Abondance).
Signposting	Good – new signposts, posts with yellow arrows on green and some faded red splashes

Mont Chauffé is an impressive rocky peak that dominates the surrounding countryside – there is a path to the top but it is steep and dangerous. This is a lovely and varied walk going round the mountain, up and over three cols, with wonderful views of the surrounding peaks. Since the snow tends to linger on the north side and the paths can be quite muddy, it is a walk better left until the summer.

The information board at the start of the walk is entitled '**Autour du Mont Chauffé**' and has a map of the walk, with details of the plants and animals you might see. Rare flowers that grow here are the edelweiss and the hairy alpenrose (*rhododendron hirsutum*), the only place in France where this is found. The mountain is home to chamois, ibex and moufflon, as well as black grouse, partridge and golden eagles.

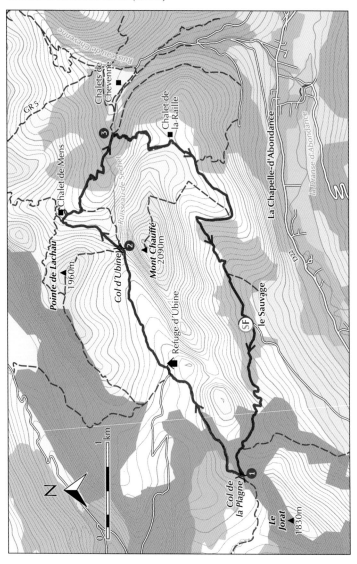

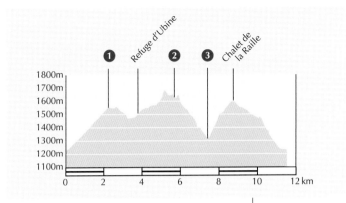

At the signpost at **le Sauvage**, take the wide stony track to the left towards Col de la Plagne/Chalets Autigny/Ubine. ▶ As you climb up this first section, you get good views of Mont de Grange across the Val d'Abondance. Keep on the main track, ignoring any paths to the left, following the yellow arrows on green. At the signpost 'les Combes – alt. 1300m', bear right, still towards Col de la Plagne, and at a further junction shortly after, bear right again. The path at first goes through coniferous forest, and then comes out into open pastures where you get your first view of the dramatic cliffs of Mont Chauffé on your right. At the signpost headed 'Alt. 1483m', where a steep track comes up from le Mont on the left, continue up to reach the **Col de la Plagne** (1546m) where there is a wooden cross and a signpost ❶ (1hr 5min). ▶

Right is where you come in at the end of the walk.

Look back here for an extended view of the Abondance valley and the high peak of Mont de Grange to the right.

You are now at the western end of the rocky cliffs of Mont Chauffé, and will start to go round its northern slopes – from here its rocky vertical peak looks particularly daunting. Turn right, signposted 'Ubine/Col d'Ubine', on an attractive undulating grassy path, with a fence on the right, through scattered firs and lovely flowers in spring, especially trumpet gentians and large purple pansies. After 10mins you leave the fence, at a post with a yellow arrow, and start to descend through woodland on a narrow path with knotted tree roots. As you come out into the open you can see the chalets of Ubine down in the valley below. The path continues to descend and, if you are doing this walk in springtime, you realise that because you are now on the north side of the mountain, the vegetation is way behind and the snow has only just left the slopes. There are carpets of little white and purple crocuses and delicate nodding bells of soldanellas, which are the first flowers to bloom after the snow. At the bottom of the hill, cross the river at a post with a yellow arrow, and walk up to the small hamlet of Ubine (1490m) (1hr 30min).

> **Ubine** is situated in a lovely open bowl, with a small chapel and some attractive old chalets, many with their original roofs of wooden tiles. The chapel of St-Bernard was built in 1798 on the site of a shrine dating from 1612, and masses were held here in summer to bless the flocks. It has been renovated twice since and contains some modern stained-glass windows.

Col d'Ubine and Mont Chauffé: photo Richard Saynor

204

The chapel at Ubine: photo Richard Saynor

Go behind the chapel to the signpost at **Ubine** and an information board on the Vallée d'Ubine, and continue through the hamlet to reach another signpost and a wooden water trough on the right, next to a refuge belonging to the Amis de la Nature (Friends of Nature) organisation (open mid June to mid September). There is also a small restaurant/bar called le Petit Champignon.

From the second signpost bear right towards Col d'Ubine/Chalets de Mens/Chalets de Chevenne. You can see the path going up towards the col, which is marked with wooden posts and crosses several small streams. You are walking up the side of a shallow valley with the towering cliffs of Mont Chauffé over on the right and Ubine down below in a sort of bowl. The gradient becomes quite steep as you get nearer to the **Col d'Ubine** (1694m), which is your second col of the day ❷ (2hr 10min).

At the signpost at the col, go straight on towards the Chalets de Mens/Chalets de Chevenne. ▶ The path traverses the hillside which drops away steeply at first, and in spring this should be negotiated with care if there

Left goes to the Pointe de Lachau.

205

Chalet overlooking the Cornettes de Bise: photo Richard Saynor

On this hillside there are spring snowflake flowers (*leucojum vernum*), which look a bit like snowdrops but have large nodding bells tipped with green.

has been heavy rain. Lower down it gets rocky in places, and there are some narrow streams to cross. As you get near the **Chalets de Mens**, it is easier to cut across right and down the hillside to reach the jeep track before the chalet. There is a good view of the Cornettes de Bise rearing up straight ahead and the cliffs of Mont Chauffé behind you. ◄ When you reach the jeep track (2hr 30min) do not turn up left (which goes to the Chalets de Mens and eventually to the Pas de la Bosse), but turn down right towards the Chalets de Chevenne, one of starting points for the Cornettes de Bise and the Lac d'Arvouin. Keep to the main jeep track down, crossing a walled alpine pasture and a stream, and then through coniferous forest with a stream, the **Ruisseau de Sechet**, below on your right.

The path bears to the left past cow pastures, and crosses the stream by a post with a yellow arrow on green. Continue downwards for about 10mins with the stream on your left until you reach a signpost to the right, headed 'Alt. 1320m' **5** (3hr).

This is the start of the third and last ascent of the day. Following the signs to la Raille par Sentier du Trapon, go

Swallowtail butterfly: photo Philip Jenkins

sharp right up a narrow path, winding steeply up into the trees towards the rocky cliffs of Mont Chauffé. The path skirts the cliffs (there is a cable along here which is not really necessary) and finally reaches a wooded dell surrounded by slopes (3hr 40min). ▶

Following a yellow arrow on a rock, take the path winding up the open hillside to the right, initially keeping the forest on your right. The path soon veers left and traverses a grassy and sometimes muddy slope, which may get washed away by snow and mud slides in spring. After 15mins you reach a wooden shrine and a signpost at **Chalet de la Raille** (1607m) (4hr).

> From **Chalet de la Raille** you get the best view of the Abondance valley below, Mont de Grange, and on the skyline the serrated peaks of the Dents du Midi with Mont Blanc just appearing behind to the left.

Turn right to reach the jeep track to the chalet and keep on this track all the way down. You pass the typical old Abondance-style farmhouses of Trosset and Crébin as the stony track continues downwards quite steeply, at first through open meadowland, and later woods and clearings. Lower down you have the impressive high rocky wall of Mont Chauffé to the right. At the signpost 'les Côtes – alt. 1280m', continue straight on through woodland to reach the parking area at **le Sauvage** (4hr 50min).

This is very attractive in summer, with numerous species of butterfly such as swallowtails, red admirals, meadow blues and tortoiseshells.

WALK 24

Roc de Tavaneuse

Start/Finish	Prétairié, Abondance valley, 1140m
Distance	8km
Total ascent	1020m
Grade	Difficult
Time	6hr
Maximum altitude	2150m
Map	IGN 3528 ET Morzine Massif du Chablais 1:25,000
Access	From Abondance, go up the main street past the shops until the road forks. Take the right fork indicating Lac de Tavaneuse, which goes alongside the Ruisseau de l'Edian, passing the Essert cable car, to the hamlet of Charmy. At Charmy follow the signs onto a narrower road to Prétairié, which consists of a large parking area and a few houses (4km from Abondance).
Signposting	Good – new signposts and where there is no signposting the way is obvious

Although long, this is a beautiful walk in an unspoiled area, with lovely flowers in springtime. The walk up to the Lac de Tavaneuse is very popular, especially in high summer, as it lies in an idyllic situation, surrounded by imposing peaks. Fewer people, however, go on to do the whole circuit as the climb up to the Roc itself is steep and exposed, but it is worth making the effort as the view of Mont Blanc and the surrounding peaks from the top is breathtaking. The descent of the Passage de Savolaire is also steep and exposed, and it is better not to do this walk if it has been raining as the rocks can be very slippery.

At the entrance to the car park there is an information board entitled 'Tavaneuse: entre eau et montagne' (between water and mountain) with a map of the walk, next to a signpost at **Prétairié** (1130m). Follow the signs to Lac de Tavaneuse/Col de Tavaneuse/Passage de Savolaire

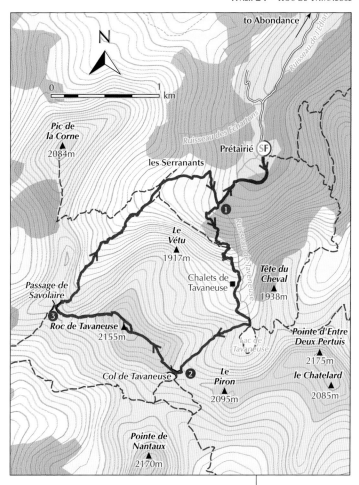

straight through the parking area onto a wide, stony jeep track. The mass of the Roc de Tavaneuse towers above as you walk along, gaining height slowly and wondering how you are ever going to get up there. You reach a signpost 'Dessus la Chargne – alt. 1250m' ❶ (25min).

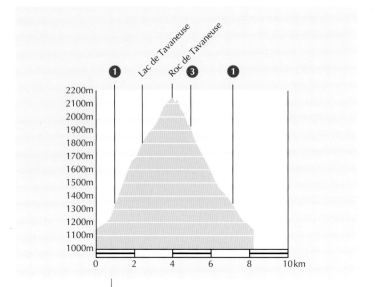

Go left towards Sous le Vétu/Chalets de Tavaneuse/ Lac de Tavaneuse (the jeep track continues to Chalets de Serranants and is the track you return from). This is a narrow path, winding steeply up the mountainside through stunted trees and scrub, and then into the open. It is rocky in places and you have to watch your footing, especially near the top where there is a cable trailing across the path. This is a well-used route and it can be slippery if it has just rained. You come to a T-junction and a signpost 'Sous le Vétu – alt. 1435m' (1hr).

Turn up left towards Chalets de Tavaneuse/Lac de Tavaneuse. The path gets rockier and steeper with a cable to help at one spot, with the **Ruisseau de Tavaneuse** on the left, and waterfalls in spring and early summer. ◄ You come to a signpost on a plateau at the **Chalets de Tavaneuse** (1683m) (1hr 50min).

Follow the path to the Lac de Tavaneuse/Col de Tavaneuse which you can see winding up the mountain in front. After a short hard grind with the stream on your

There is an imposing view back to Prétairié and the Cornettes de Bise on the right.

left, you arrive at the **Lac de Tavaneuse** (1805m), a picturesque little lake nestling in a valley with high mountain slopes all around it (2hr 15min).

At the signpost 'Lac de Tavaneuse', follow signs to Col de Tavaneuse/Roc de Tavaneuse up towards the next signpost on the pass ahead. Keep to the higher path round the end of the lake, rather than the lower more undefined path that goes along the valley bottom (both join up later on). The higher path traverses the slope and then goes steeply up to the **Col de Tavaneuse ❷** (1997m). Here there are spectacular views, with the Mont Blanc massif on the horizon (3hr).

Follow the sign right to the Roc de Tavaneuse. The path goes over the top of the ridge and is quite exposed; in autumn the slopes here are covered in heather. When you reach the end at a big rock, climb up right to the **Roc de Tavaneuse** itself, where there is a big wooden cross (3hr 30min).

Wintry view of the Dents du Midi from the Roc de Tavaneuse: photo Sharon Bryand

From the **Roc de Tavaneuse** there are magnificent views of the nearby Mont de Grange, Dent d'Oche,

Cornettes de Bise and Mont Chauffé, with Mont Blanc and the Dents du Midi further away. On a clear day you can even see as far as the Vanoise.

Retrace your steps downwards for about 70 metres and take the first turning left – careful, as there is no signpost or splash here. The path goes round the back of the Roc de Tavaneuse and you get an impressive view of the rock face as the path goes round the steep slope and then up to a ridge (3hr 50min).

At the top bear right and keep on the narrow path as it undulates along a long, exposed, grassy ridge (there is a cross on a hump to the right) to reach a signpost at the **Passage de Savolaire** (1930m) ❸ (4hr 20min).

The **Passage de Savolaire** is a long, steep path heading down into the valley towards les Serranants. Take care here as if the ground is wet this can be very slippery. To the left are the precipitous peaks of the Pointe de Savolaire, Mont Brion and the Roc d'Enfer.

As you get lower the path becomes rockier, and you come to a signpost 'Combe de Savolaire – alt. 1600m' where you continue straight on towards les Serranants/ Prétairié (5hr). After the signpost the track becomes easier and you can see the buildings of les Serranants ahead. Continue down until you reach a further signpost at **les Serranants** (1430m) just above the chalet (5hr 20min).

Continue straight on towards Prétairié and soon after you reach the jeep track going to the chalets and the signpost 'les Serranants (Chalets) – alt. 1403m'. Continue down the wide jeep track to reach the signpost at Dessus la Chargne ❶, which you passed on the way up, and walk back to the car park at **Prétairié** (6hr).

WALK 25

Mont de Grange

Start/Finish	Chapelle St-Théodule, 1325m
Distance	13.5km
Total ascent	1145m
Grade	Strenuous
Time	6hr 15min
Maximum altitude	2430m
Map	IGN 3528 ET Morzine Massif du Chablais 1:25,000
Access	From Abondance, take the road towards Lac des Plagnes through Sur-la-Fontaine and Sur-la-Ravine, then bear left towards Follebin and Chapelle St-Théodule, and bear left again at Follebin. There is limited parking at the end of the tarmac road, 500 metres before the chapel, otherwise continue up the stony dirt road and park just beyond the chapel, next to a fountain and an information board on the Réserve du Mont de Grange.
Signposting	Good – new signposts and red/white markings for the short distance on the GR5

The Mont de Grange is one of the highest peaks in the Val d'Abondance and dominates the whole valley. The views at the summit are outstanding, with a 360-degree panorama in all directions. The walk up is long and strenuous, and is one of the few in this guide that goes up and down the same way. The Mont de Grange is a nature reserve, so you have a good chance of seeing chamois, ibex and, if lucky, the elusive moufflon, introduced in 1969. When in the reserve, dogs must be kept on a lead.

From **Chapelle St-Théodule**, take the stony track on the right of the information board, which is a continuation of the road you drove up. Shortly after, take the left fork to a small shrine, the Oratoire des Trables, and a signpost. Follow signs to le Covillet/Chalets du Bailly/Lenlevay on a path that goes steeply up into woods. It crosses a small

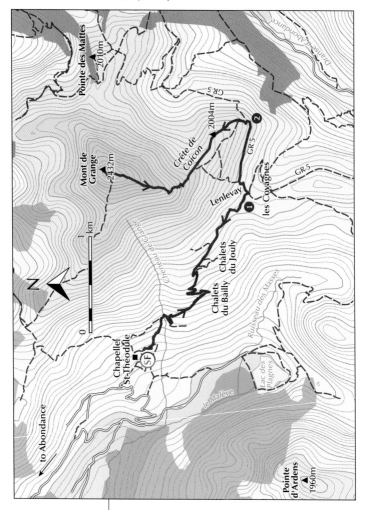

stream, the **Cheneau de Grange**, and continues steeply uphill to reach the open again at the Chalet du Covillet (1430m) (20min).

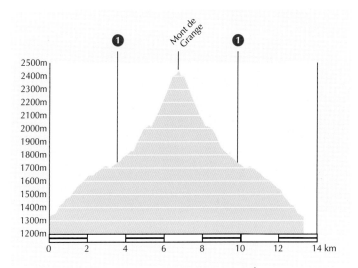

At the chalet turn left, towards Chalets du Bailly/
Lenlevay, and go back into woods to the signpost at
Chalets du Bailly (1540m). Continue on towards le Jouly
Bas/Lenlevay. The track now becomes less steep and
goes through open pastureland where Abondance cows
are grazing. Ignore a track on the left, which leads to a
barn, and continue straight on. You soon reach the farmhouse at **le Jouly Bas** (1640m) and then come to **le Jouly
Haut** (1689m) (1hr 10min). Continue upwards through
open pastureland to reach a crossroads and a signpost
at **Lenlevay** (1733m), where the GR5 comes in ❶ (1hr
25min). ▸

From here, you look
across to the peaks of
the Dents du Midi.

Turn left on the GR5 (red/white markings), following the signs to l'Etrye, passing some chalets and a large
cowshed. Just beyond the cowshed look for a wooden
sign indicating Mont de Grange and follow the jeep track
up until you reach the signpost on the left headed 'Alt.
1840m' ❷ (1hr 50min). Here you leave the red/white
markings of the GR5, which continues straight on to
l'Etrye and the Pointe des Mattes.

215

Sheep blocking the path to the summit: photo Richard Saynor

The distinctive grassy peak of the Pointe des Mattes is on the right, and in the valley below you can see the Lac des Plagnes, with Mont Blanc and the Dents du Midi on the horizon.

Go up left following signs to Mont de Grange par l'Arête de Coicon. The narrow path zigzags steeply up through stunted alder and raspberry bushes (keep right where path diverts) and onto the long grassy ridge of the **Crête de Coicon**. Continue steeply up, keeping to the left of the ridge until you reach a cairn, and then cross to the other side. ◄ After the ridge you reach a rocky area which you climb through to reach the summit of **Mont de Grange** (2432m) (3hr 45min).

> **Mont de Grange** is one of the highest peaks in the Chablais and the views are literally breathtaking. The orientation table shows all the mountains you can see on a clear day, as far away as the Gran Paradiso in northern Italy and the Bernese Oberland in Switzerland. There is also an iron cross on the summit, and further on a range of solar panels and radio masts.

Retrace your steps, and when you get down from the ridge at the signpost at ❷ turn right. Continue to reach Lenlevay ❶ and again turn right here and follow all signs to Oratoire les Trables, which will take you back to the car (6hr 15min).

WALK 26

Pointe des Mattes

Start/Finish	Très-les-Pierres, Châtel, 1180m
Distance	10.5km
Total ascent	890m
Grade	Strenuous
Time	4hr 50min
Maximum altitude	2005m
Map	IGN 3528 ET Morzine Massif du Chablais 1:25,000
Access	From Abondance, take the D22 through Chapelle d'Abondance to Châtel, the last village before the road goes over the Pas de Morgins into Switzerland. Just after the church in Châtel, go down to the right on the D228A towards Linga/Prè-la-Joux (straight on leads into Switzerland). About 3.5km from the church, you come to the Auberge de Jeunesse de Montagne on the left side of the road, and a blue/white sign on the right at Route de Pré-la-Joux/Chemin de la Cascade, by a signpost 'Très-les-Pierres – alt. 1160m'. Turn right between two chalets into the Chemin de la Cascade and drive up to the small chapel where there is a parking area on the left.
Signposting	Good – new signposts, wooden posts with yellow arrows and red/white markings for the GR5

This is a lovely walk in the Mont de Grange nature reserve, where you might see marmots, herds of chamois and moufflons if you are quiet. The higher Mont de Grange dominates the walk, and there are impressive views of the other peaks of the Chablais, including the Dents du Midi in Switzerland.

The **Chapelle de Très-les-Pierres** was built in 1784, and dedicated to St François de Sales, the 16th-century priest sent to convert the Haute Savoie back to Catholicism after the Reformation. When the chapel was renovated in 2011, a small sealed

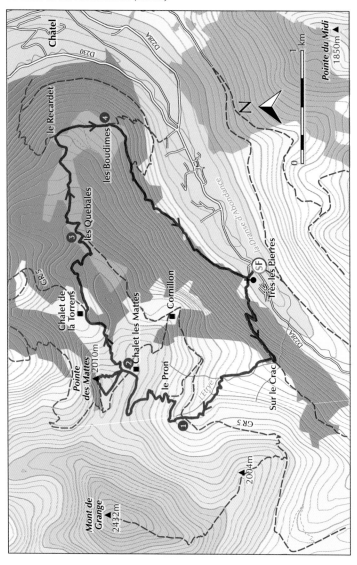

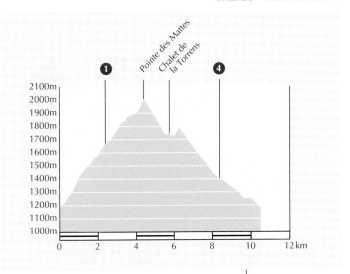

casket was found buried under the altar, which X-rays revealed to contain a piece of elbow bone. Tests are being held to see if this could belong to St François himself.

Go straight up past the **chapel** and a large rock on the right to an information board about the Réserve du Mont de Grange, and a signpost at **Très-les-Pierres** (1180m). Go left towards Sur le Crac/Canyon de Cornillon/l'Etrye/ les Mattes. ▶ The wide stony track winds steeply upwards through woodland, with tall rocky cliffs to the right and wooded slopes left, past the signpost at Canyon de Cornillon, to reach the next signpost at **Sur le Crac** (1450m) (50min).

To the right is where you will come in at the end of the walk.

Turn right following the sign indicating l'Etrye/les Mattes to reach an attractive open grassy bowl. Keep to the grassy path with fir trees to the left, passing a track on the right leading to the farm of l'Arête. Ahead is the Col de la Corne, with the Pointe des Mattes to the right and the much higher slopes of Mont de Grange (2432m) to the left. The path crosses a stream where there is a chalet up on the right, winding up grassy slopes full of yellow gentians in summer, and past trees with brightly coloured leaves in autumn. Keep straight on (do not go down right) to cross the stream again higher up, and shortly after you reach a junction and a signpost at **Ruisseau de l'Etrye** (1660m) ❶ (1hr 35min).

From here you get a good view of the serrated peaks of the Dents du Midi and the Portes du Soleil skiing area on the other side of the valley.

Following the sign to le Pron/les Mattes, turn off the main track onto a narrow grassy path which winds steeply up the hillside over open pastures. You have now joined the red/white signs of the GR5, which came in from the left. ◄ The path crosses a small waterfall and a few streams to reach the three cow barns at **le Pron** (1741m) (1hr 50min).

Following the signs to les Mattes/Chalet de la Torrens, continue upwards to reach a T-junction where you bear right at a post and red/white GR sign and walk along the contour of the slope, a welcome relief after the previous steepness, to the **Chalet les Mattes**. Continue to the signpost just past the chalet ❷ (2hr 30min).

Dents du Midi from les Mattes

It takes about 15mins to climb the grassy slope to the summit of the **Pointe des Mattes**, 110m higher – be

careful here as the ridge falls away very abruptly (2hr 45min).

Steep slopes of the Pointe des Mattes from the Chalet de la Torrens

The summit of **Pointe des Mattes** is an ideal spot for a picnic and to enjoy the extended view of the surrounding mountains. Mont de Grange towers overhead, with the Cornettes de Bise and Mont Chauffé on the other side of the Val d'Abondance, and the Dents du Midi and les Diablerets directly opposite.

Walk along the ridge from the summit to get the best views, and then bear left to descend to the signpost at ❷. Turn left following signs to Chalet de la Torrens/les Crottes/les Boudimes. This is a fairly steep path down, where you have to watch your feet as it skirts the rocky cliffs of the Tête de la Torrens and descends into a grassy valley, where cows are grazing. Lower down it gets easier, but the path can be muddy if it has been raining. Keep following the red/white GR markings, and the occasional post with yellow arrows on green, to reach the signpost at

Chalet de la Torrens (1735m), which is a small cowshed (3hr 15min).

Go straight on towards les Quebales/les Boudimes/ Très-les-Pierres par les Boudimes (here the red/white GR markings go off left to les Crottes). You are now on a wider track, which goes down and then up again, through coniferous forest and open pastureland, to reach the signpost at **les Quebales** (1790m) ❺. From this high point you can look back for a good view of the Pointe des Mattes with the higher Mont de Grange looming behind it. Following the signs to les Boudimes, continue on down the wide track, with lovely views of the Val d'Abondance valley, to reach the signpost 'les Quebales Bas – alt. 1720m' (3hr 35min).

Continue down towards les Boudimes/Très-les-Pierres, going underneath pylon wires and keeping on the wide main track. ◀ At the signpost at **le Recardet** you are starting to turn round the mountain and the valley is now on the left. Continue on the same wide track, going steadily downwards through fir trees and then open pastureland to reach the scattered chalets of **les Boudimes** ❹ (4hr 15min).

There is a good view of Châtel in the valley below and a little lake with a fountain, a miniature of the Jet d'Eau in Geneva.

Go straight on towards Très-les-Pierres, ignoring all paths to the left. The track drops down steeply through forest and over a number of streams flowing down from the mountainside, passing further signposts. Keep on the forest track, which is now flatter, passing more attractive waterfalls spilling over the rock face and across the track to the valley below. You reach the signposts at the start of the walk, just behind the chapel and your car (4hr 50min).

WALK 27
Le Morclan

Start/Finish	Le Tenne, near Petit Châtel, 1305m
Distance	11.5km
Total ascent	730m
Grade	Medium
Time	4hr 30min
Maximum altitude	1980m
Map	IGN 3528 ET Morzine Massif du Chablais 1:25,000
Access	From Abondance, take the D22 to Châtel, the last village in France before the road goes over the Pas de Morgins into Switzerland. In the centre of Châtel, opposite the church, turn up left and then left again at a sign saying Petit Châtel. Drive up this narrow road past hotels and chalets until you get to Petit Châtel (1250m) and then turn right by the signpost indicating Col de Conches/ Morgins. The road goes under the chairlift and continues up. Leave your car on the side of the road before the first hairpin bend where there is a signpost 'le Tenne – alt. 1308m'.
Signposting	Good – new signposts and posts with yellow arrows on green (some signs removed from September to May)

Despite the number of ski-tows on these slopes, this is a spectacular walk with the ascent of two summits, both with outstanding views of Mont Blanc and the surrounding peaks in France and Switzerland – on a clear day you can see as far as the Eiger, Mönch and Jungfrau in the Bernese Oberland. The dramatic ridge between the summits follows the border between France and Switzerland, crossing the route used in the past by smugglers. In summer the slopes are covered with alpenrose and other flowers, and you might see ibex or moufflon, or even a golden eagle circling overhead.

From **le Tenne**, go up the road which soon deteriorates into a jeep track. At the signpost at the next hairpin bend,

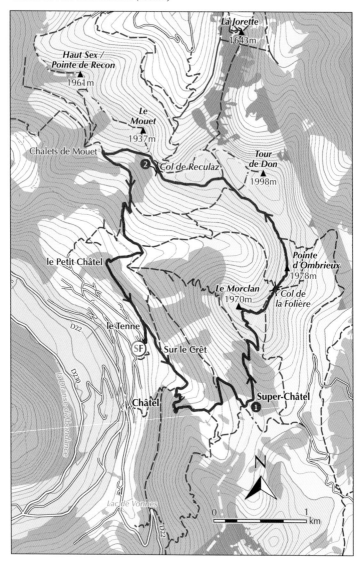

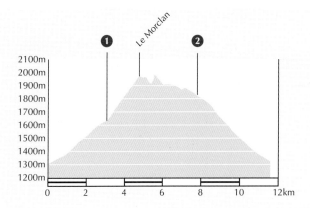

headed 'Alt. 1325m', turn right towards Sur le Crêt/ Super-Châtel. ▸ Stay on the wide jeep track and ignore other paths branching off. There is a chairlift ahead with a cable car beyond. After 10mins continue straight past the signpost at **Sur le Crêt** on the jeep track, going under la Combe chairlift through open meadowland, bearing round the right of the mountain. ▸ Where possible take the obvious short cuts as you zigzag up this track (some of them have been closed off as VTT trails), going under the cable car opposite a bar/restaurant called 'les Portes au Soleil' and the start of the Téléski les Coqs (45min).

After the restaurant bear left on the jeep track. The track goes under the cable car, past the sign headed 'l'Ortaz – alt. 1600m', and under the chairlift again before arriving at the buildings of **Super-Châtel** ❶ with lifts in all directions. Continue on the jeep track, past the restaurant/hotel 'Escale Blanche Relais de Gourmand' and the cable car building on the right, to reach a signpost on the left by some chalets (1hr 15min).

Bear up left, following the sign to Le Morclan, under the chairlift and up the slope to the right to reach a jeep track. Turn left at the signpost here and stay on the steep track which soon passes under a ski-tow and heads towards the chairlift up to Le Morclan. Bear left to stay

Left is where you come out at the end of the walk.

There is a beautiful view to the right over the Val d'Abondance and you can see the huddle of huts of Sur le Crêt below.

If you look back there is a lovely view down to Châtel and the Dranse valley, dominated by Mont de Grange.

on the jeep track where the track divides. At the signpost 'Sous le Morclan – alt. 1830m', turn right towards Le Morclan. ◄ Continue up to reach the summit of **Le Morclan** (1970m) (2hr).

> On **Le Morclan** there is a stone cairn and two orientation tables giving the names of the surrounding peaks and the animals and birds to look out for, including the ibex and golden eagle. You can see the Dents du Midi and the Mont Blanc massif when you are facing southwest, and the Eiger, Mönch and Jungfrau on the horizon if you are looking to the northeast. To the left of the summit are large TV antennae and to the right is the top of the chairlift. In summer the slopes all around are covered with alpenrose and globeflowers, with a few rare yellow bellflowers (*campanula thyrsoides*).

Orientation table at the summit:
photo Richard Saynor

Continue to the right and walk along the ridge, passing the top of the chairlift to reach a small wooden hut and a yellow Swiss signpost (keep to the top path rather than the lower jeep track, although they meet up later on). This is the border between France and Switzerland, and there are old stones dating back to 1891 marking the frontier. The path soon dips down about 60m to the **Col de la Folière** (1908m), one of the routes used in the past by smugglers.

There is a story that one dark night a group of **smugglers**, laden with haunches of ham bound for Switzerland, were heading for this col when they heard the sound of the customs men lying in wait for them. They quickly threw their merchandise into holes in the snow at the foot of some fir trees, and then convinced their interlocutors that they were simply taking a stroll to enjoy the moonlight on the ridge. In the absence of proof, the customs men escorted the smugglers back to the village where they were released. But when they scurried back to retrieve their hidden contraband the next day, they found that it had been eaten by foxes – justice had been done!

The path then climbs up again to undulate along a rather airy ridge, with a spectacular view ahead of the Rhône valley and the eastern end of Lake Geneva, with the towns of Montreux and Vevey on the far shore. Continue to **Pointe des Ombrieux**, the highest point of

The airy ridge from Pointe des Ombrieux: photo Richard Saynor

227

the walk, and then to Portes d'Onnaz. After descending a final slope on the ridge, a ski-tow comes up from the right by another yellow Swiss signpost indicating **Tour de Don** (2hr 40min), a green hump over on the right 20mins away.

Keep straight ahead on the path, which goes round a green bowl with farms down below. You are walking through open grassland just under the ridge on the French side, and for much of the way there is a fence and the old border stones. You see two huts over on the right – one is Chaux Longe, which is the end of a ski-tow coming up from Switzerland, and further on you walk beneath another tow starting down on the left, named 'Contrebandiers' (smugglers) after the smuggling at this border. Soon after there is a signpost headed 'Alt. 1870m' indicating Chalets du Mouet 40mins, and you can see buildings at the top of another ski-tow from Switzerland over on the right. At the signpost 'Tête de Tronchet – alt. 1860m' keep straight on towards the Col de Reculaz (also called the Col de Croix). Follow this jeep track under the Barbossine chairlift to reach the **Col de Reculaz** ❷ (3hr 10min).

Continue straight on, towards the Col de Recon, even though the signpost indicates Châtel left – there is also a path coming up from the Swiss side. The track descends below a chalet bypassing two iron gates, and then past two more buildings to a T-junction at a signpost at **Chalets de Mouet** (3hr 30min). ◄

The large building up to the right is the Buvette de Mouet, if you need refreshment.

Go down left, towards Barbossine, and follow this main jeep track for about an hour, passing various signposts which are alternative routes that you should ignore. The track zigzags down and circles round the bottom of the Barbossine chairlift at the point where it connects with the end of the Petit Châtel chairlift. At the signpost 'Barbossine dessous – alt. 1460m', bear left towards la Tenne and continue down through woodland to reach the hairpin bend and the signpost at the start of the walk. Walk down the road to your car (4hr 30min).

VAL DE MORZINE

Looking towards the Roc d'Enfer from the Col de Chésery (Walk 28)

The Val de Morzine follows the third tributary of the River Dranse, which flows almost due south between the other two. The walks in this valley are all in the upper reaches of the river near its source, to the south of the Val d'Abondance.

If you follow this branch of the Dranse up from Bioge, you pass through the village of St-Jean d'Aulps where the 12th-century Cistercian monastery, now in ruins, once owned all the surrounding lands, including Morzine itself. The inhabitants produced crops and livestock for the monastery until its destruction in 1531 during the Reformation, after

which they were free to farm the land for themselves. However, it was not nearly as fertile as in the nearby Val d'Abondance, and despite some income from slate mining, the village remained a quiet backwater until 1862 when a road was constructed linking it with Thonon. Gradually tourism began to develop, and the first hotel was built in 1925, followed by the first ski lift in 1934. Since then the town has gone from strength to strength, especially since the 1970s when the higher resort of Avoriaz was constructed and the Portes du Soleil ski complex established, linking 12 resorts in France and Switzerland.

Dents du Midi from the Col de Cou (Walk 30)

Morzine is now a lively town in both summer and winter, and has managed to retain a certain charm, with some old chalets in the centre. It is easily accessible from both the north and the south, and has plenty of accommodation, with more than 50 hotels as well as several campsites.

The town is surrounded by high mountains, and not all of them are marred by ski installations. Dominating it to the south is the Pointe de Ressachaux, a little visited peak which provides a spectacular viewpoint over Morzine and Avoriaz. To the east are lovely walks up to the lakes and high cols on the Swiss border, once used by smugglers between France and Switzerland, as were the cols above Châtel in the Val d'Abondance and above Samoëns in the Haut Giffre. The most beautiful walks are up to the cols above the Lac de Montriond and the smaller Lac des Mines d'Or, and to the Col de Brétolet, just over the border, where there is an ornithological station monitoring the thousands of birds which migrate over here every spring and autumn.

The driving directions for walks in this section are from Morzine.

WALK 28

Col de Chésery

Start/Finish	Les Lindarets, 1495m
Distance	12.5km
Total ascent	590m
Grade	Medium
Time	4hr 30min
Maximum altitude	1995m
Map	IGN 3528 ET Morzine Massif du Chablais 1:25,000
Access	From Morzine, take the D228 to Montriond, and then, still on the D228, follow signs to Lac de Montriond/ les Lindarets. The road goes past the Lac de Montriond on the right and on to les Lindarets. In the middle of the village turn right at the Restaurant les Rhodos and go all the way through the village to les Marmottes bar/ restaurant. Turn left into this wide shallow valley and park just beyond les Marmottes, at the Chaux Fleurie chairlift.
Signposting	Mostly good – new signposts, posts with yellow arrows on green and red/white markings for the GR5 between the Col de Chésery and the Col de Bassachaux

Apart from the initial climb up to the Col de Chésery, this is an easy balcony walk between a lake and two cols, with lovely views down to the Lac de Montriond and, at the Col de Bassachaux, towards the Val d'Abondance and Mont de Grange. In early summer the slopes are bright with flowering alpenrose, and in autumn with the russet coloured leaves of bilberries.

Les Lindarets is a busy little place in summer and winter, with numerous chalet-type restaurants. It is known as the village of goats, as in summer these wander around freely, and anything that can be made from goatskin is on sale in the shops. In winter it is one of the 12 resorts of the Portes du Soleil

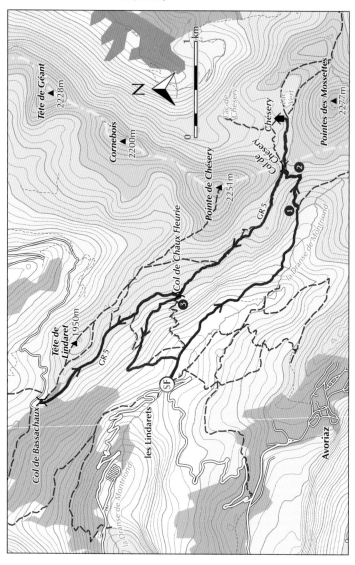

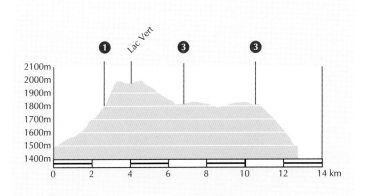

ski complex, with several chairlifts and ski-tows
linking the slopes between France and Switzerland.

From the wooden signpost 'les Marmottes', take the wide
jeep track up the valley towards the Col de Chésery,
passing under the Chaux Fleurie chairlift. After 5mins
you reach the signpost 'la Lécherette – alt. 1520m'. Go
straight on, towards Cascade des Brochaux. ▶

The track going up
to the left, indicating
Col de Chésery, is the
way you will return.

After about 20mins you reach another signpost 'les
Brochaux – alt. 1585m', just before the chairlift of les
Mossettes. Turn left towards Col de Chésery/Lac Vert, and
continue up this wide jeep track through lovely alpine
pasture.

In summer there are a **variety of flowers** covering
the meadows, including lots of marsh orchids, cotton grass and bird's eye primula where the ground
is damp, with alpenrose, gentians, pulsatilla anemones, moss campion, martagon lilies and several
species of orchids as you get higher.

Continue on the jeep track for about another 40mins,
until the point where the chairlift is closest to the track
and there is a large rock on the left, with Chésery and an

The chairlift up to Col de Chésery

arrow painted on it in yellow. Note that there is no signpost here, where you would expect one ❶ (1hr).

Follow the arrow left towards Chésery (the jeep track goes straight on to the south, to the Pas de Cuboré and the Pas de Chavanette). This is a narrow but well-defined path that goes steeply uphill under the chairlift, and then bears to the right across slopes of alpenrose. After about 30mins it bears to the left to reach the **Col de Chésery** (1992m), which sits on the French-Swiss border. Here there is no French signpost, only a standard yellow Swiss one ❷ (1hr 45min).

Follow the sign to the right, to Refuge de Chésery/ Lac Vert/Pointe des Mossettes. You are now on the GR5, marked by the usual red/white signs, and in Switzerland. It takes about 15mins to the **Refuge de Chésery**, which overlooks the attractive **Lac Vert** (1972m), a small green-coloured lake nestling in a bowl in the mountains. You can see the GR5 continuing round the left side of the lake and over the top of another pass.

The **terrace of the refuge** is perfectly situated for a drink and a rest to contemplate the lake and surrounding scenery. It is a very popular spot in summer, especially at weekends, as it is a staging post on the GR5.

The Refuge de Chésery-Lac Vert, **www.lacvert.ch**, has dormitory accommodation for 24 people, and serves meals and drinks. It is open from June to October.

Following the GR signs, retrace your path back to the signpost at the Col de Chésery ❷ (2hr 20min) and follow the signs to Montriond/Col de Bassachaux/Châtel. This is a clearly marked balcony path, still on the **GR5**, undulating along the side of the mountain with the track visible a long way ahead. At several places there are signs indicating that walkers should keep to the left and mountain bikers (VTT) to the right on the slightly wider track. The peaks on the other side of the valley are dotted with ski lifts.

In early summer the **slopes** are bright with alpenrose, trumpet gentians and globe flowers, and in autumn with purple heather and russet-coloured bilberry bushes – this is the time when the local farmers pick the small blue berries which are then made into jam or tarts.

After about 30mins you see the top of the Chaux Fleurie chairlift up on the right, and then the path goes underneath an electricity wire to a signpost at **Col de Chaux Fleurie** (1800m) ❸ (2hr 50min). ▶ Go straight on towards the Col de Bassachaux. The path now widens into a level jeep track going through occasional coniferous trees and crossing rivulets of water, if the weather has been wet. There are lovely views to the left of the Lac de Montriond, with the surrounding peaks reflected in its deep blue water. Walk under the Chaux Fleurie chairlift and then cross a ski trail to a junction off to the

You will return to this signpost for the descent to les Lindarets.

right where there is a chalet selling Abondance cheese (*Abondance en Vente*). A few minutes later there is a signpost headed 'la Lambe – alt. 1820m' and another path up to the right, towards Pointe de Chésery/Crêtes des Rochassons.

> Here is the first of several **information boards** along the track to the Col de Bassachaux, with illustrations of the various birds found in the area – nutcracker, wheatear, ring ousel, citril finch, black grouse, wagtail, dipper and spotted woodpecker, among others.

Continue straight on round the mountain to reach the **Col de Bassachaux** (3hr 20min). There are usually lots of cars and people when you arrive since it is accessible from Châtel in the Val d'Abondance, and has a picnic area and a well-frequented restaurant.

> The **Col de Bassachaux** is a lovely place to stop as there is a wonderful panorama down the Val d'Abondance to Châtel, and one of the best uninterrupted views of Mont de Grange (2432m). Beyond the restaurant are two orientation tables where you can identify the different peaks.
>
> There are also several interesting information boards here, in both French and English: on the creation of the Lac de Montriond by a rockfall; the glaciation of the valley; the dynamics of mountain streams; the history of Mont de Grange; and, in the grounds of the restaurant at the Oratoire de Gros Robin, on the smuggling which took place in these mountains on the French-Swiss border, mostly at night or in bad weather to avoid the customs men. Cattle and dried meat were traded by the French, in return for tobacco, coffee, spices and sugar by the Swiss. There is a small museum on the history of smuggling on this border in the Val d'Abondance, near Châtel.

Retrace your steps for about 20mins to the signpost at the Col de Chaux Fleurie ❸ and go down the wide jeep track, following the signs to les Lindarets. Note the signpost here indicates 1hr 10min to les Lindarets, but this is clearly wrong as shortly after there is another signpost indicating 35min; in actual fact it takes about 40mins from the first signpost. Stay on the jeep track where there are signs to the left for mountain bikers, and continue down, going underneath the chairlift in the direction of the Col de Bassachaux, only lower down, before doubling back down to the valley at the signpost at la Lécherette. Turn right to reach your car in **les Lindarets** (4hr 30min).

Janette Norton walking towards the Col de Bassachaux, with Mont de Grange ahead

WALK 29
Pointe de Ressachaux

Start/Finish	La Grangette, Morzine, 1050m
Distance	7.5km
Total ascent	1145m
Grade	Strenuous
Time	5hr 15min
Maximum altitude	2170m
Map	IGN 3528 ET Top 25 Morzine Massif du Chablais 1:25,000
Access	From Morzine, take the D338 towards Avoriaz and just outside the town, cross the bridge, making for the church. At the end of the bridge turn right, signposted to Vallée de la Manche and Télépherique Nyon/ Charmossière. Drive by the start of the Télépherique Nyon, and then take the first turning sharp back left at la Grangette onto the Route de la Mernaz. Park on the left, about 400 metres along this road, just past a large wooden chalet called le Ressachaux and opposite a wooden signpost 'la Mernaz – alt. 1065m'. If the limited parking here is full, use the official parking of the Télépherique Nyon on the road below and follow the signs to Ressachaux, about 100m uphill.
Signposting	Good in parts – old wooden signposts and yellow circles

The Pointe de Ressachaux dominates the town of Morzine and looks very imposing from afar. The long and strenuous climb to the summit is unrelentingly steep, and the path up the grassy shoulder to the top is quite exposed to the elements. From the summit you get a bird's-eye view of the ski resort of Morzine-Avoriaz and a 360-degree panorama, including the nearby high peaks of Hauts Forts, with Mont Blanc in the distance.

From the signpost 'la Mernaz', follow signs 'Pointe de Ressachaux 2hr 30min/le Creux 1hr 30min' (this is

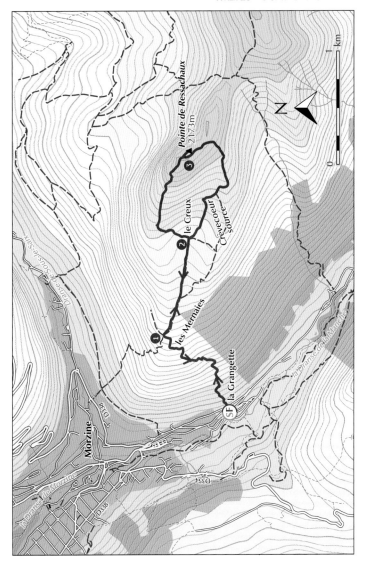

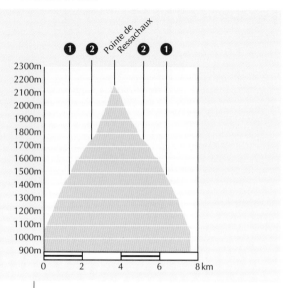

optimistic). The path is narrow and immediately goes up steeply through tall coniferous and beech trees, with yellow circles to show the way. Keep on the main path, which is well trodden but rocky, with lots of tree roots to negotiate – it is steep all the way. You reach a clearing and vestiges of a chalet called **les Mernaies**, consisting of a few stone walls and some tumbledown wooden beams. From here the path is less steep for a while, with more open woodland. Keep on the main track, ignoring a red cross on a rock and a narrower path going up right, to reach a crossroads and signpost 'le Cmon – alt. 1530m' ❶ (1hr).

Turn right towards le Creux, still on the main path (yellow and red marking on a rock and wooden arrows). The path passes a picnic table and a couple of small wooden chalets and comes out into open pastureland, with a good view of the Morzine valley below and the Plénay cable car on the other side of the valley. Continue straight up on a grassy path past another hut called le

The rustic water trough at le Creux: photo Richard Saynor

Plianday, renovated in 2001. The path then goes fairly steeply up through wild raspberry and alder bushes, with the peak of the Ressachaux visible ahead. You can see the long steep shoulder you have to go up, which looks rather daunting. The path takes you to **le Creux** (1760m) (1hr 40min) ❷.

> In **le Creux** there are a number of small huts dotted about and an old wooden water trough with a somewhat incongruous stainless steel pipe dispensing delicious cool water. There is a seat here too where you can take a well-earned rest before tackling the second part of the ascent.

At the water trough bear left towards the visible path going up the side of the slope. After skirting round the buildings, the path climbs steeply up through open meadowland and bushes onto the shoulder of the mountain.

In June the **slopes** are covered with pulsatilla anemones and trumpet gentians, and in high summer there are lots of tall yellow and purple monkshood, feathery purple adenostyles with big green leaves, cornflowers, scabious and astrantia. On the left there is a clear view of the village of Morzine in the valley below.

Now begins the long ascent up the grassy shoulder of the mountain – it seems to go on forever! The path is quite exposed to the elements, with a precipitous drop on the left, but nothing to worry about. Where the path divides about 100 metres before the summit ❸, take the left fork up the rocks to the **Pointe de Ressachaux** (2173m) (3hr).

Ridge before the summit of the Pointe de Ressachaux: photo Philip Jenkins

An imposing **granite cross** was erected on the summit in 2016. The inscription, in the Savoyard language and French, is a prayer to the ancestors of those living in the valley, who worked hard to provide milk for their families. From here you can

clearly see the buildings and ski installations of Morzine-Avoriaz, and further round are the peaks of Hauts Forts, at 2466m the highest in the valley, and Mont Blanc.

Retrace your steps to the fork at ❺ and go left on a narrow path which skirts round the mountain below the rocky summit. It then traverses steeply round to the left and descends the shoulder of the southern flank of the mountain. Watch your feet here, as the path may be slippery when wet. From here you can see the path going right down to the huts of le Creux. ▸ Continue downwards on the defined path, clearly marked with yellow circles, to reach a wooden signpost (1857m) at the **source of the Crèvecoeur** stream (3hr 30min).

There are lovely views straight ahead of the Môle and the Pointe de Marcelly, and to the left you can see the Tête de Bostan above Samoëns.

Follow the rocky streambed down, and then go through alder bushes and vegetation to reach the bottom of the combe by a rock. In autumn, you may detect a whiff of aniseed in the air, which probably emanates from the many fennel plants which grow here. The path continues past scattered huts to reach the water trough at **le Creux** ❷.

From here retrace your steps to the crossroads at ❶ and bear left, following signs to la Mernaz, back to your car just before **la Grangette** (5hr 15min).

WALK 30
Col de Cou

Start/Finish	Lac des Mines d'Or, near Morzine, 1390m
Distance	10km
Total ascent	735m
Grade	Medium
Time	4hr 30min
Maximum altitude	1990m
Map	IGN 3530 ET Samoens Haut-Giffre 1:25,000
Access	From Morzine, follow the signs to Avoriaz at the end of the village and then turn right, indicated Vallée de la Manche/Lac des Mines d'Or/Télépherique Nyon/Charmossière. Go along this narrow road, past the télépherique, until the very end (7km) and park in the car park by the Lac des Mines d'Or.
Signposting	Good – new signposts, yellow splashes on the way up and red/white GR5 signs for most of the way down

This is a delightful walk from a small lake up to two high cols. The Col de Cou is on the border between France and Switzerland, and in former times this was a well-known smugglers' route between the two countries, and in the Second World War a crossing point for both refugees and partisans. The nearby Col de Bretolet in Switzerland has an ornithological observatory, built in 1958, and both cols are renowned as routes for thousands of migrating birds in spring and autumn. If you do the walk in early autumn, you can watch the ornithologists catching the birds in nets in order to monitor them as they fly south.

At the **Lac des Mines d'Or** there is an information board which explains that the lake was artificially created in 1981, and is named after the gold mines higher up the mountain which were dug by the Swiss in 1850. Only a little gold was found and the mines were soon abandoned, with the shafts now

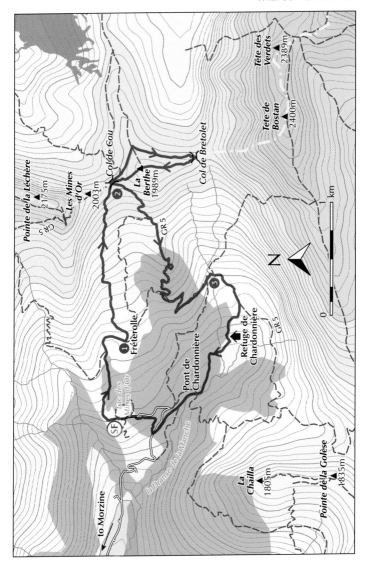

245

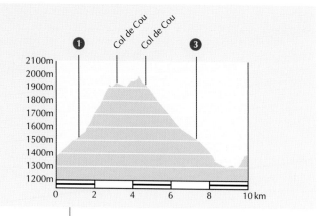

blocked by rockfalls. The lake is attractively set in a bowl in the mountains, and there is a pleasant stroll around it taking about 10 minutes. It is now a popular tourist site, with a hotel and restaurant, a children's play area and donkeys for hire.

From the car park, walk up to a No Entry sign leading onto a wide jeep track through tall fir trees. Follow this for about 15mins to the end of the trees and a signpost 'le Charnier – alt. 1506m'. Continue straight on, over open grassy slopes, following the signs to Chalets de Fréterolle/Col de Cou until you reach **Fréterolle** (30min).

At **Fréterolle** there is a mountain café where you can buy drinks, meals and freshly made cheeses, and an information board on the birds of the region. These include golden eagle, peregrine falcon, black grouse, kestrel, alpine chough, nutcracker, black redstart, wheatear, raven and water pipit.

At the signpost next to this board ❶ take the narrow path up to the left, indicating 'Col de Cou par les Alpages'. (Do not go straight on, indicated 'Col de Cou par la fôret'.) The path steadily gains height over grassy slopes with cows grazing. ▸ Continue upwards over the open slopes towards the col, which you can see ahead of you. You finally reach the **Col de Cou** (1920m) where there is a small hut which was originally the French-Swiss customs post, a border stone dated 1891 and yellow Swiss signposts ❷ (1hr 45min).

At the **Col de Cou** there is a spectacular view into Switzerland. A panorama board names all the mountains you can see, the most dramatic being the serrated teeth of the Dents du Midi, with the snow-covered Mont Ruan to its right, and les Diablerets to the left; ahead you look down over the ski slopes of Champéry.

In spring and summer look out for gentians, alpenrose, different species of orchids and other alpine flowers. In a mild autumn, trumpet gentians can be found in flower even as late as November.

Resting on the Col de Cou border stone

Walking towards the Col de Bretolet and the Tête de Boston: photo Sharon Bryand

To reach the Col de Bretolet, take the path towards Planachaux/Champéry for about 100 metres to a yellow Swiss signpost indicating straight on to Barme/Berroi, and shortly after turn off to the right on an unsigned track. This leads round the back of the ridge to a yellow Swiss signpost headed 'Alt. 1931m'. You can now see the huts of the observatory ahead, so turn right and walk along the side of the hill, through banks of bilberry and alder bushes, to reach the **Col de Bretolet** (1936m) (2hr 10min).

During the **migration period** in early autumn, nets are strung up to the right and left of the col to catch the birds, and it is interesting to watch the ornithologists as they carefully take the birds out of the nets to be identified, weighed and ringed before being released to continue their journey. Over 20,000 birds of 100 different species are caught here, and it is a sobering thought that of thousands that fly over the pass every autumn, only half survive to make the return journey the following spring. If they are

Watching migrating birds on the Col de Bretolet

not too busy, the ornithologists will happily talk to you about their task, and you may also find other bird watchers here with their binoculars, hoping to spot a rare species.

Just before the observatory building, a narrow path bears up to the right alongside the nets (only there in the migration period) and winds up the ridge to reach the highest point at **La Berthe** (1989m). From here you descend to return to the Col de Cou ❷ (2hr 40min).

From the Col de Cou, turn left on the wider track, which is the **GR5**. Follow the red/white GR markings down to the signpost at Epingly where you continue straight on, following the signs to the Refuge de Chardonnière. This leads down the shoulder of the mountain and enters forest as you zigzag lower. ▶ At the signpost 'Chardonnière – alt. 1600m', go left, towards Refuge de Chardonnière (3hr 20min). Continue down on a track flanked by bracken and wild rhubarb, through dense pine forest and past a gate, to reach a signpost 'Torrent de

To the left is the dramatic wall of les Terres Maudits, ahead is the Col de la Golèse and to the right across the valley is the Pointe de Ressachaux.

249

Chardonnière' on a corner. There is also a noticeboard here with a map showing the Tour des Dents Blanches ❺ (3hr 35min).

Go straight on following the GR signs. (Do not take the wider jeep track to the right which is a shorter way back to the lake.) Cross a stream and go through a gate on to another wide track. Further down you emerge into attractive meadowland and come to a sign 'Plan des Heures – alt. 1460m'. Over on the left is where the GR5 splits off to go to the Refuge de la Golèse. Continue downwards on a jeep track into scattered forest. As you come round a corner, you can see the **Refuge de Chardonnière** ahead on your left. This is an attractive chalet and a good place for a drink and a rest (3hr 55min).

> The Refuge de Chardonnière, **www.refuge-chardonniere.fr**, has accommodation for 20 in two dormitories, with showers and hot water, and serves meals and drinks. It is open from mid June to mid September.

Turn right towards Pont de Chardonnière and continue down the jeep track. Cross a stream, and then go through tall coniferous trees and a picnic area to reach the **Pont de Chardonnière**, where there is a large information board. Cross the bridge and follow the signs to le Charny par la Fôret. This is a pleasant walk through trees to reach the road. Cross this to a signpost indicating Lac des Mines d'Or, 10min. This is a fairly steep path in the woods, which leads up to the car park at the **Lac des Mines d'Or** (4hr 30min).

APPENDIX A
Route summary table

Walk no	Name	Distance	Time	Total ascent/descent	Grade	Page
Salève and Vuache						
1	Gorges du Salève	9km	4hr 15min	690m	Medium	44
2	Balcon du Salève	7km	2hr	170m	Easy	52
3	Grand Piton	9.5km	3hr 45min	630m	Medium	57
4	Pointe du Plan	10km	4hr	590m	Medium	64
5	Boucle de l'Iselet	10.5km	3hr 15min	345m	Easy	71
6	Le Vuache	7.5km	3hr	520m	Easy	77
Vallée Verte						
7	Signal des Voirons	12km	4hr 45min	785m	Medium	85
8	Mont de Vouan	8km	3hr 15min	455m	Medium	95
9	Pointe de Miribel	13km	4hr 45min	790m	Medium	101
10	Montagne d'Hirmentaz	9.5km	4hr	550m	Medium	108
11	Mont Forchat	13.5km	5hr 20min	800m	Medium	113
Vallée du Brevon						
12	Mont d'Hermone	10.5km	4hr	685m	Medium	122
13	Rocher de Nifflon	9km	4hr 30min	760m	Medium	129
14	Pointe de la Gay	12km	5hr	830m	Medium	137

Walk no	Name	Distance	Time	Total ascent/descent	Grade	Page
15	Pointe de Chalune	12km	6hr	1000m	Strenuous	144
16	Haute Pointe	10km	4hr 45min	810m	Medium	151
17	Pointe d'Uble	10km	5hr	785m	Medium	157
Pré-Alpes du Léman						
18	Pic des Mémises	11km	4hr 45min	780m	Medium	165
19	Pic Boré	10km	5hr	885m	Strenuous	171
20	Dent d'Oche	7.5km	5hr 45min	960m	Difficult	177
Val d'Abondance						
21	Cornettes de Bise	12.5km	7hr 15min	1235m	Difficult	188
22	Lac d'Arvouin	10.5km	4hr 45min	725m	Medium	195
23	Autour du Mont Chauffé	11.5km	4hr 50min	870m	Strenuous	201
24	Roc de Tavaneuse	8km	6hr	1020m	Difficult	208
25	Mont de Grange	13.5km	6hr 15min	1145m	Strenuous	213
26	Pointe des Mattes	10.5km	4hr 50min	890m	Strenuous	217
27	Le Morclan	11.5km	4hr 30min	730m	Medium	223
Val de Morzine						
28	Col de Chésery	12.5km	4hr 30min	590m	Medium	231
29	Pointe de Ressachaux	7.5km	5hr 15min	1145m	Strenuous	238
30	Col de Cou	10km	4hr 30min	735m	Medium	244

APPENDIX B
Useful information

Tourist information

Official website of tourism in France
http://uk.france.fr

Official website for the Haute Savoie
www.savoie-mont-blanc.com

Specific sites
Note that these are prone to change due to departmental or local reorganisation

Abondance
www.abondance.org

Bellevaux
www.alpesduleman.com

Chapelle d'Abondance
www.lachapelle74.com

Châtel
www.chatel.com

Cruseilles
www.cruseilles.fr

Evian-les-Bains
www.evian-tourisme.com

Morzine
www.morzine-avoriaz.com

St-Julien-en-Genevois
www.st-julien-en-genevois.fr

Thollon-les-Mémises
www.thollonlesmemises.com

Thonon-les-Bains
www.thononlesbains.com

Vallée Verte
www.alpesduleman.com

Printed maps

1:25,000 (1cm = 250m)
For the walking trails, the IGN Cartes de Rando Top 25 Série Bleu maps usually show the paths clearly, but it is important to get the most recent editions. The following are used in this guide:

Map	Walk(s)
3330 OT Bellegarde-sur-Valserine	6
3428 ET Thonon/Evian	11,12,13
3429 ET Bonneville/Cluses	7, 8, 9, 10, 14, 15, 16, 17
3430 OT Mont Salève/St-Julien-en-Genevois	1, 2, 3, 4, 5
3528 ET Morzine/Massif du Chablais	18, 19, 20, 21, 22, 23, 24, 25, 26, 27, 28, 29
3530 ET Samoëns/Haut Giffre	30

1:100,000 (1cm=1km)

IGN Top 100 Tourisme et Découverte No.144 Annecy/Thonon-les-Bains – gives an overall picture of the Haute Savoie walking areas

1:200,000 (1cm=2km)
Michelin 523 Rhône-Alpes – a good road map of the region

Bookshops

Most large English bookshops with a travel section should sell these maps, or they can be ordered from the official French IGN website (www.ign.fr) which always has the most recent editions; from Amazon (www.amazon.co.uk); or from the following specialist shops: Stanfords (www.stanfords.co.uk), The Map Shop (www.themapshop. co.uk) or Cordee (www.cordee.co.uk). In France, local bookshops, newsagents and big supermarkets also stock maps.

Market days

Below is a list of market days in the towns and villages mentioned in this guide. Although they attract many tourists, these markets are in general aimed at the local population so they start early and finish around lunch-time. They offer a wide range of goods and home-grown produce, with stalls laden with different cheeses, cold meats, bread, fruit and home-grown vegetables, as well as wine, honey and often clothes. Markets are good places to pick up regional specialities for your picnic lunch. There are also *foires* in the larger towns, often linked with the seasons. Many are agricultural fairs, exhibiting livestock and equipment, while others have stalls with regional products, arts and crafts, clothes, books or bric-a-brac. Some date back to the 1800s, and a few even as far back as the Middle Ages. One of these is the Autumn Fair in Abondance, which has been held on the first Sunday in October since 1424. It marks the return of the cows from the alpine pastures, and is mainly a cattle and cheese fair.

Monday	Bellevaux, Thonon, Viuz-en-Sallaz
Tuesday	Boëge, Evian-les-Bains
Wednesday	Châtel, Frangy, Morzine
Thursday	Taninges, Thonon-les-Bains
Friday	Chapelle d'Abondance, Evian-les-Bains, St Jeoire, St-Julien-en-Genevois
Saturday	Saint-Paul
Sunday	Abondance, Collonges-sous-Salève

APPENDIX C
Glossary of useful French words

French	English
aigle	eagle
aiguille	needle-like peak
alpage	summer pasture
arbre	tree
arête	ridge
au bout de	at the end of (something)
balade	short walk
bas	low
batons	trekking poles
bolet	type of mushroom
borne	boundary marker (usually concrete)
boucle	circle or loop (used to describe a round trip)
bourg	market town
bouquetin	ibex
brouillard	fog
buvette	small café
cailloux	stones, rocks
carrefour	crossroads
carte	map
cascade	waterfall
chambre d'hôte	bed and breakfast
chapelle	chapel
champignon	mushroom
chemin	path
cheval	horse
chèvre	goat

French	English
chute de pierre	rockfall
ciel	sky
clairière	clearing, glade
col	pass, saddle
combe	shallow valley
commune	district (small)
couloir	corridor or narrow passageway through rocks
coup de soleil	sunstroke
crête	ridge
croix	cross
danger (dangereux)	danger (dangerous)
descendre	to go down
église	church
entrée interdite	no entry
est	east
étang	pond
falaise	cliff
ferme	farm
foudre	lightning
fleur	flower
gouffre	large hole, chasm
grimper	to climb
grotte	grotto
hameau	hamlet
haut/e	high
herbe	grass
là-bas	down there
là-haut	up there
lac	lake

French	English
mairie	town hall
marcher (se promener)	to walk
météo	weather forecast
montagne	mountain
monter	to go up
moraine	debris (rocks) carried down by a glacier
moulin	mill
mouton	sheep
neige	snow
névé	snow patch
nord	north
nuage (nuageux)	cloud (cloudy)
oiseau	bird
orage	thunderstorm
oratoire	wayside shrine
ouest	west
papillon	butterfly
parcours vita	exercise route (usually in woods)
pèlerin	pilgrim
pente	slope, gradient
pic	peak or summit (also means woodpecker)
pierre	stone
piste	track (usually meaning a man-made path for skiers)
pluie	rain
pointe	point or peak (eg Pointe de la Gay)
pont	bridge
poteau (indicateur)	signpost
pré/praz	meadow
propriété privée	private property

French	English
randonnée	long walk
ravin	ravine, gully
refuge	mountain hut
renard	fox
rivière	river
rocher	rock
route	road
ruisseau	stream or rivulet
sac à dos	rucksack
sac de couchage	sleeping bag
sanctuaire	sanctuary
sapin	fir tree
sentier	marked path
serpent	snake
soleil	sun
sommet	summit
source	spring (water)
sud	south
taureau	bull
télécabine	cable car
télésiège	chairlift
téléski	drag, tow or pommel lift
tempête	thunderstorm
temps	weather
tonnerre	thunder
trou	hole
vache	cow
vallée	valley
versant	side (of a mountain)

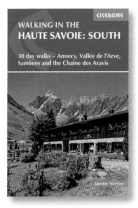
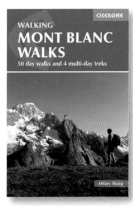
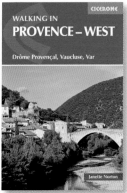

DOWNLOAD THE ROUTE
IN GPX FORMAT

All the routes in this guide are available for download from:

www.cicerone.co.uk/810/GPX

as GPX files. You should be able to load them into most formats of mobile device, whether GPS or smartphone.

When you go to this link, you will be asked for your email address and where you purchased the guide, and have the option to subscribe to the Cicerone e-newsletter.

www.cicerone.co.uk

LISTING OF CICERONE GUIDES

SCOTLAND
Backpacker's Britain:
     Northern Scotland
Ben Nevis and Glen Coe
Cycling in the Hebrides
Great Mountain Days in Scotland
Mountain Biking in Southern and
     Central Scotland
Mountain Biking in West and
     North West Scotland
Not the West Highland Way
Scotland
Scotland's Best Small Mountains
Scotland's Far West
Scotland's Mountain Ridges
Scrambles in Lochaber
The Ayrshire and Arran
     Coastal Paths
The Border Country
The Cape Wrath Trail
The Great Glen Way
The Great Glen Way Map Booklet
The Hebridean Way
The Hebrides
The Isle of Mull
The Isle of Skye
The Skye Trail
The Southern Upland Way
The Speyside Way
The Speyside Way Map Booklet
The West Highland Way
Walking Highland Perthshire
Walking in Scotland's Far North
Walking in the Angus Glens
Walking in the Cairngorms
Walking in the Ochils, Campsie
     Fells and Lomond Hills
Walking in the Pentland Hills
Walking in the Southern Uplands
Walking in Torridon
Walking Loch Lomond and
     the Trossachs
Walking on Arran
Walking on Harris and Lewis
Walking on Jura, Islay
     and Colonsay
Walking on Rum and the
     Small Isles
Walking on the Orkney and
     Shetland Isles
Walking on Uist and Barra
Walking the Corbetts
     Vol 1 South of the Great Glen
Walking the Corbetts
     Vol 2 North of the Great Glen
Walking the Galloway Hills

Walking the Munros
     Vol 1 – Southern, Central and
     Western Highlands
Walking the Munros
     Vol 2 – Northern Highlands
     and the Cairngorms
West Highland Way Map Booklet
Winter Climbs Ben Nevis and
     Glen Coe
Winter Climbs in the Cairngorms

NORTHERN ENGLAND TRAILS
Hadrian's Wall Path
Hadrian's Wall Path Map Booklet
Pennine Way Map Booklet
The Coast to Coast Map Booklet
The Coast to Coast Walk
The Dales Way
The Pennine Way

LAKE DISTRICT
Cycling in the Lake District
Great Mountain Days in the
     Lake District
Lake District Winter Climbs
Lake District: High Level and
     Fell Walks
Lake District: Low Level and
     Lake Walks
Lakeland Fellranger series
Mountain Biking in the
     Lake District
Scrambles in the
     Lake District – North
Scrambles in the
     Lake District – South
Short Walks in Lakeland
     Books 1, 2 and 3
The Cumbria Coastal Way
The Cumbria Way
Tour of the Lake District
Trail and Fell Running in the
     Lake District

**NORTH WEST ENGLAND
AND THE ISLE OF MAN**
Cycling the Pennine Bridleway
Isle of Man Coastal Path
The Lancashire Cycleway
The Lune Valley and Howgills –
     A Walking Guide
The Ribble Way
Walking in Cumbria's Eden Valley
Walking in Lancashire
Walking in the Forest of Bowland
     and Pendle
Walking on the Isle of Man

Walking on the West
     Pennine Moors
Walks in Lancashire
     Witch Country
Walks in Ribble Country
Walks in Silverdale and Arnside
Walks in the Forest of Bowland

**NORTH EAST ENGLAND,
YORKSHIRE DALES
AND PENNINES**
Cycling in the Yorkshire Dales
Great Mountain Days in
     the Pennines
Historic Walks in North Yorkshire
Mountain Biking in the
     Yorkshire Dales
South Pennine Walks
St Oswald's Way and
     St Cuthbert's Way
The Cleveland Way and the
     Yorkshire Wolds Way
The Cleveland Way Map Booklet
The North York Moors
The Reivers Way
The Teesdale Way
Walking in County Durham
Walking in Northumberland
Walking in the North Pennines
Walking in the Yorkshire Dales:
     North and East
Walking in the Yorkshire Dales:
     South and West
Walks in Dales Country
Walks in the Yorkshire Dales

WALES AND WELSH BORDERS
Glyndwr's Way
Great Mountain Days
     in Snowdonia
Hillwalking in Shropshire
Hillwalking in Wales – Vol 1
Hillwalking in Wales – Vol 2
Mountain Walking in Snowdonia
Offa's Dyke Path
Offa's Dyke Map Booklet
Pembrokeshire Coast Path
     Map Booklet
Ridges of Snowdonia
Scrambles in Snowdonia
The Ascent of Snowdon
The Ceredigion and Snowdonia
     Coast Paths
The Pembrokeshire Coast Path
The Severn Way
The Snowdonia Way

The Wales Coast Path
The Wye Valley Walk
Walking in Carmarthenshire
Walking in Pembrokeshire
Walking in the Forest of Dean
Walking in the South
  Wales Valleys
Walking in the Wye Valley
Walking on the Brecon Beacons
Walking on the Gower
Welsh Winter Climbs

DERBYSHIRE, PEAK DISTRICT AND MIDLANDS

Cycling in the Peak District
Dark Peak Walks
Scrambles in the Dark Peak
Walking in Derbyshire
White Peak Walks:
  The Northern Dales

SOUTHERN ENGLAND

20 Classic Sportive Rides in
  South East England
20 Classic Sportive Rides in
  South West England
Cycling in the Cotswolds
Mountain Biking on the
  North Downs
Mountain Biking on the
  South Downs
North Downs Way Map Booklet
South West Coast Path Map
  Booklet – Minehead to St Ives
South West Coast Path Map
  Booklet – Plymouth to Poole
South West Coast Path Map
  Booklet – St Ives to Plymouth
Suffolk Coast and Heath Walks
The Cotswold Way
The Cotswold Way Map Booklet
The Great Stones Way
The Kennet and Avon Canal
The Lea Valley Walk
The North Downs Way
The Peddars Way and Norfolk
  Coast Path
The Pilgrims' Way
The Ridgeway Map Booklet
The Ridgeway National Trail
The South Downs Way
The South Downs Way
  Map Booklet
The South West Coast Path
The Thames Path
The Thames Path Map Booklet
The Two Moors Way
Walking in Cornwall
Walking in Essex
Walking in Kent

Walking in London
Walking in Norfolk
Walking in Sussex
Walking in the Chilterns
Walking in the Cotswolds
Walking in the Isles of Scilly
Walking in the New Forest
Walking in the North
  Wessex Downs
Walking in the Thames Valley
Walking on Dartmoor
Walking on Guernsey
Walking on Jersey
Walking on the Isle of Wight
Walking on the Jurassic Coast
Walks in the South Downs
  National Park

BRITISH ISLES CHALLENGES, COLLECTIONS AND ACTIVITIES

The Book of the Bivvy
The Book of the Bothy
The C2C Cycle Route
The End to End Cycle Route
The End to End Trail
The Mountains of England and
  Wales: Vol 1 Wales
The Mountains of England and
  Wales: Vol 2 England
The National Trails
The UK's County Tops
Three Peaks, Ten Tors

ALPS CROSS-BORDER ROUTES

100 Hut Walks in the Alps
Across the Eastern Alps: E5
Alpine Ski Mountaineering
  Vol 1 – Western Alps
Alpine Ski Mountaineering Vol 2
  – Central and Eastern Alps
Chamonix to Zermatt
The Tour of the Bernina
Tour of Mont Blanc
Tour of Monte Rosa
Tour of the Matterhorn
Trail Running – Chamonix and
  the Mont Blanc region
Trekking in the Alps
Trekking in the Silvretta and
  Rätikon Alps
Trekking Munich to Venice
Walking in the Alps

PYRENEES AND FRANCE/SPAIN CROSS-BORDER ROUTES

The GR10 Trail
The GR11 Trail – La Senda
The Mountains of Andorra
The Pyrenean Haute Route
The Pyrenees

The Way of St James – France
The Way of St James – Spain
Walks and Climbs in the Pyrenees

AUSTRIA

The Adlerweg
Trekking in Austria's Hohe Tauern
Trekking in the Stubai Alps
Trekking in the Zillertal Alps
Walking in Austria

SWITZERLAND

Cycle Touring in Switzerland
The Swiss Alpine Pass Route –
  Via Alpina Route 1
The Swiss Alps
Tour of the Jungfrau Region
Walking in the Bernese Oberland
Walking in the Valais
Walks in the Engadine –
  Switzerland

FRANCE

Chamonix Mountain Adventures
Cycle Touring in France
Cycling the Canal du Midi
Écrins National Park
Mont Blanc Walks
Mountain Adventures in
  the Maurienne
The Cathar Way
The GR20 Corsica
The GR5 Trail
The GR5 Trail – Vosges and Jura
The Grand Traverse of the
  Massif Central
The Loire Cycle Route
The Moselle Cycle Route
The River Rhone Cycle Route
The Robert Louis Stevenson Trail
Tour of the Oisans: The GR54
Tour of the Queyras
Tour of the Vanoise
Vanoise Ski Touring
Via Ferratas of the French Alps
Walking in Corsica
Walking in Provence – East
Walking in Provence – West
Walking in the Auvergne
Walking in the Cevennes
Walking in the Dordogne
Walking in the Haute Savoie:
  South
Walks in the Cathar Region
Walking in the Ardennes

GERMANY

Hiking and Biking in the
  Black Forest
The Danube Cycleway Volume 1

The Rhine Cycle Route
The Westweg
Walking in the Bavarian Alps

ICELAND AND GREENLAND

Trekking in Greenland
Walking and Trekking in Iceland

IRELAND

The Irish Coast to Coast Walk
The Mountains of Ireland

ITALY

Italy's Sibillini National Park
Shorter Walks in the Dolomites
Ski Touring and Snowshoeing in
    the Dolomites
The Way of St Francis
Through the Italian Alps
Trekking in the Apennines
Trekking in the Dolomites
Via Ferratas of the Italian
    Dolomites: Vol 1
Via Ferratas of the Italian
    Dolomites: Vol 2
Walking in Abruzzo
Walking in Italy's Stelvio
    National Park
Walking in Sardinia
Walking in Sicily
Walking in the Dolomites
Walking in Umbria
Walking on the Amalfi Coast
Walking the Italian Lakes
Walks and Treks in the
    Maritime Alps

SCANDINAVIA

Walking in Norway

EASTERN EUROPE
AND THE BALKANS

The Danube Cycleway Volume 2
The High Tatras
The Mountains of Romania
Walking in Bulgaria's
    National Parks
Walking in Hungary
Mountain Biking in Slovenia
The Islands of Croatia
The Julian Alps of Slovenia
The Mountains of Montenegro
Trekking in Slovenia
Walking in Croatia
Walking in Slovenia:
    The Karavanke

SPAIN

Coastal Walks in Andalucia
Cycle Touring in Spain

Mountain Walking in
    Southern Catalunya
Spain's Sendero Histórico:
    The GR1
The Mountains of Nerja
The Northern Caminos
The Sierras of Extremadura
The Way of St James
    Cyclist Guide
Trekking in Mallorca
Walking in Andalucia
Walking in Mallorca
Walking in Menorca
Walking in the
    Cordillera Cantabrica
Walking in the Sierra Nevada
Walking on Gran Canaria
Walking on La Gomera and
    El Hierro
Walking on La Palma
Walking on Lanzarote
    and Fuerteventura
Walking on Tenerife
Walking on the Costa Blanca
Walking the GR7 in Andalucia
Walks and Climbs in the
    Picos de Europa

PORTUGAL

Walking in Madeira
Walking in the Algarve

GREECE

The High Mountains of Crete
Walking and Trekking on Corfu

CYPRUS

Walking in Cyprus

MALTA

Walking on Malta

INTERNATIONAL CHALLENGES,
COLLECTIONS AND ACTIVITIES

Canyoning in the Alps
The Via Francigena
    Canterbury to Rome – Part 2

AFRICA

Climbing in the Moroccan
    Anti-Atlas
Kilimanjaro:
    A Complete Trekker's Guide
Mountaineering in the Moroccan
    High Atlas
The High Atlas
Trekking in the Atlas Mountains
Walking in the Drakensberg

ASIA

Jordan – Walks, Treks, Caves,
    Climbs and Canyons
Treks and Climbs in Wadi Rum,
    Jordan
Annapurna
Everest: A Trekker's Guide
Trekking in the Himalaya
Bhutan
Trekking in Ladakh
The Mount Kailash Trek

NORTH AMERICA

British Columbia
The Grand Canyon
The John Muir Trail
The Pacific Crest Trail

SOUTH AMERICA

Aconcagua and the
    Southern Andes
Hiking and Biking Peru's
    Inca Trails
Torres del Paine

TECHNIQUES

Geocaching in the UK
Indoor Climbing
Lightweight Camping
Map and Compass
Outdoor Photography
Polar Exploration
Rock Climbing
Sport Climbing
The Hillwalker's Manual

MINI GUIDES

Alpine Flowers
Avalanche!
Navigation
Pocket First Aid and
    Wilderness Medicine
Snow

MOUNTAIN LITERATURE

8000 metres
A Walk in the Clouds
Abode of the Gods
The Pennine Way – the Path,
    the People, the Journey
Unjustifiable Risk?

For full information on all our
guides, books and eBooks,
visit our website:
www.cicerone.co.uk

Walking – Trekking – Mountaineering – Climbing – Cycling

Over 40 years, Cicerone have built up an outstanding collection of over 300 guides, inspiring all sorts of amazing adventures.

Every guide comes from extensive exploration and research by our expert authors, all with a passion for their subjects. They are frequently praised, endorsed and used by clubs, instructors and outdoor organisations.

All our titles can now be bought as **e-books**, **ePubs** and **Kindle** files and we also have an online magazine – **Cicerone Extra** – with features to help cyclists, climbers, walkers and trekkers choose their next adventure, at home or abroad.

Our website shows any **new information** we've had in since a book was published. Please do let us know if you find anything has changed, so that we can publish the latest details. On our **website** you'll also find great ideas and lots of detailed information about what's inside every guide and you can buy **individual routes** from many of them online.

It's easy to keep in touch with what's going on at Cicerone by getting our monthly **free e-newsletter**, which is full of offers, competitions, up-to-date information and topical articles. You can subscribe on our home page and also follow us on **Facebook** and **Twitter** or dip into our **blog**.

Cicerone – the very best guides for exploring the world.

CICERONE

Juniper House, Murley Moss, Oxenholme Road, Kendal, Cumbria LA9 7RL
Tel: 015395 62069 info@cicerone.co.uk
www.cicerone.co.uk and **www.cicerone-extra.com**